ॐ

# श्रीमद्भगवद्गीता

## द्वादशोऽध्यायः – भक्तियोगः

# śrīmadbhagavadgītā

## dvādaśo'dhyāyaḥ - bhaktiyogaḥ

ॐ

# Bhagavad-Gītā Chapter Twelve

**Sanskrit Text with Transliteration, Translation & Brief Commentary**

ॐ

# गीता मूलं १२

## Gītā Mūlaṁ 12

— ॐ —

गीता या मधुसूदनप्रभविणी युक्ता परं ब्रह्मणि
gītā yā madhusūdana-prabhaviṇī yuktā paraṁ brahmaṇi
या कृष्णेन कृताऽखिलं नयनवद् वक्षोऽतिगूढार्थिनी ।
yā kṛṣṇena kṛtā-'khilaṃ nayanavad vakṣo-'tigūḍhārthinī ,
या लोकत्रयस्य मार्गविधिनी धर्मस्य साक्षात्पथा
yā lokatrayasya marga-vidhinī dharmasya sākṣāt-pathā ,
सा श्रीकृष्णमुखारविन्दजनिता तस्याः मूलं प्रयच्छामि ॥
sā śrī-kṛṣṇa-mukhāravinda-janitā tasyāḥ mūlaṁ prayacchāmi .

That Gītā—which's born from Madhusūdana -- who exists in Oneness with Braham;
that Gītā—which's uttered by Krishna -- of profound visions of deep mysteries concealed within;
that Gītā—which lights the Dharma-path across the threefold world;
that Gītā—that sprung from Shri Krishna's lotus-lips
—to Her sacred roots I proceed and take refuge.

— ॐ —

Belongs to ____________________

॥ यतो धर्मस्ततो जयः - एकं-सनातन-धर्म विजयः ॥

- yato dharmastato jayaḥ -- ekaṁ sanātana-dharma vijayaḥ -

- Where Dharma abides Victory abides -- Victory unto Ekam-Sanātana-Dharma -

Published by: only **RAMA** only

*Title:* **Gita Mulam 12 – Bhagavad Gita Chapter Twelve**
*Sub-Title:* **Sanskrit Text with Transliteration, Translation & Brief Commentary**
A No-Opinions Commentary. Only Facts. Bhagavad-Gita As It Truly Is.
An Excellent Resource for Sectless Gita-Study (With Wide Margin for Taking Notes)

**गीता मूलं १२**
**gītā mūlaṁ 12**
**श्रीमद्भगवद्गीता द्वादशोऽध्यायः – भक्तियोगः**
**śrīmadbhagavadgītā dvādaśo'dhyāyaḥ - bhaktiyogaḥ**

*Authors:* Adarsh Saxena & Vijay Kumar

Identifiers

ISBN: 978-1-945739-52-1 (Paperback)

—o—

**Coming Soon:**
- Gita Mūlaṁ 01 – Bhagavad Gita Chapter One
- Gita Mūlaṁ 02 – Bhagavad Gita Chapter Two
- Gita Mūlaṁ 03 – Bhagavad Gita Chapter Three
- Gita Mūlaṁ 04 – Bhagavad Gita Chapter Four
- Gita Mūlaṁ 05 – Bhagavad Gita Chapter Five (Available, ISBN: 978-1-945739-75-0)
- Gita Mūlaṁ 06 – Bhagavad Gita Chapter Six
- Gita Mūlaṁ 07 – Bhagavad Gita Chapter Seven
- Gita Mūlaṁ 08 – Bhagavad Gita Chapter Eight
- Gita Mūlaṁ 09 – Bhagavad Gita Chapter Nine
- Gita Mūlaṁ 10 – Bhagavad Gita Chapter Ten
- Gita Mūlaṁ 11 – Bhagavad Gita Chapter Eleven
- Gita Mūlaṁ 12 – Bhagavad Gita Chapter Twelve (Available, ISBN: 978-1-945739-52-1)
- Gita Mūlaṁ 13 – Bhagavad Gita Chapter Thirteen
- Gita Mūlaṁ 14 – Bhagavad Gita Chapter Fourteen
- Gita Mūlaṁ 15 – Bhagavad Gita Chapter Fifteen (Available, ISBN: 978-1-945739-51-4)
- Gita Mūlaṁ 16 – Bhagavad Gita Chapter Sixteen (Available, ISBN: 978-1-945739-76-7)
- Gita Mūlaṁ 17 – Bhagavad Gita Chapter Seventeen
- Gita Mūlaṁ 18 – Bhagavad Gita Chapter Eighteen

**[All 18 books in this Gita Mūlaṁ series (for each chapter of the Bhagavad-Gitā) will become available by Fall 2026]**

—o—

Our Bhagavad-Gitā Books:

**Bhagavad Gita, The Holy Book of Hindus, with Sanskrit Text, English Translation & Transliteration, No Commentary.**
- **-ISBN: 978-1-945739-36-1 / 978-1-945739-37-8** (Paperback/Hardback. Book Size 6.14"x9.21"x190 pages)
- **-ISBN: 978-1-945739-39-2** (For Gitā Journaling. 8"x8"x390 pages)
- **-ISBN: 978-1-945739-43-9** (Convenient Pocket-Sized Edition. 4"x6"x180 pages)
- **-ISBN: 978-1-945739-40-8** (Legacy Book. 7.5"x9.25"x246 pages)
- **-ISBN: 978-1-945739-55-2 / 978-1-945739-56-9** (Paperback/Hardback. For Note-Taking. 7.5"x9.25"x190 pages)

Also Available:
- **Tulsi Ramayana—Hindu Holy Book:** Ramcharitmanas with English Translation (ISBNs: 978-1-945739-**60-6**, 978-1-945739-**61-3**)
- **Ramcharitmanas - Large/Medium/Small** (No Translation)
- **Sundarakanda:** The Fifth-Ascent of Tulsi Ramayana (ISBNs: 978-1-945739-**05-7**, 978-1-945739-**15-6**)
- **Rama Hymns:** Hanuman-Chalisa, Rāma-Raksha-Stotra, etc. (ISBNs: 978-1-945739-**25-5**, 978-1-945739-**09-5**):
- **Vivekachudamani, Fiery Crest-Jewel of Wisdom** (ISBNs: 978-1-945739-**44-6**, 978-1-945739-**45-3**, 978-1-945739-**41-5**)
- **Ashtavakra Gītā, the Fiery Octave** (ISBNs: 978-1-945739-**46-0**, 978-1-945739-**47-7**, 978-1-945739-**42-2**)
- **Legacy Books - Endowment of Devotion (several):** Journal Books of sacred Hindu Hymns around which the Holy-Name Rama Name can be written; available in Paperback and Hardcover for: **Hanuman Chalisa** (ISBN: 1945739274/ 1945739940) **Sundara-Kanda** (ISBN: 1945739908/ 1945739916) **Rama-Raksha-Stotra** (ISBN: 1945739991/ 1945739967) **Bhushundi-Ramayana** (ISBN: 1945739983/ 1945739975) **Nama-Ramayanam** (ISBN: 1945739304/ 1945739959)
- **Rama Jayam - Likhita Japam Rama-Nama Mala alongside Sacred Hindu Texts (several):** Books for writing the 'Rama' Name 100,000 Times. Rama Jayam - Likhita Japam:Rama-Nama Mala. Available in Book Size 8"x10" (Paperback) for: **Hanuman Chalisa** (ISBN: 1945739169) **Rama Raksha Stotra** (ISBN: 1945739185) **Nama-Ramayanam** (ISBN: 1945739045) **Ramashtakam** (ISBN: 1945739177) **Rama Shatanama Stotra** (ISBN: 1945739266) **Rama-Shatnamavalih** (ISBN: 1945739134) **Simple (I)** (ISBN: 1945739142)
- **Likhita Japam -** Paperback books for writing the 'Rama' Name in dotted grids: **One-Lettered Rama Mantra**, Book Size 8"x10" (ISBN: 1945739312) **Two-Lettered Rama Mantra,** Book Size 8"x10" (ISBN: 1945739320) **Three-Lettered Rama Mantra,** Book Size 8"x10" (ISBN: 1945739339) **Four-Lettered Rama Mantra,** Book Size 8"x10" (ISBN: 1945739347) **Simple (II)** Book Size 7.5"x9.25" (ISBN: 1945739193) **Simple (III)** Book Size 8"x8" (ISBN: 1945739282) **Simple (IV)** Book Size 8.5"x8.5" (ISBN: 1945739878) **Simple (V)** Book Size 8.5"x11" (ISBN: 1945739924)

# CONTENTS

# गीता मूलं १२
## gītā mūlaṁ 12
## श्रीमद्भगवद्गीता द्वादशोऽध्यायः – भक्तियोगः
## śrīmadbhagavadgītā dvādaśo'dhyāyaḥ - bhaktiyogaḥ

# bhagavad-gītā

## श्रीमद्भगवद्गीता

### प्रथमोऽध्यायः - अर्जुनविषादयोगः

*धृतराष्ट्र उवाच –*

धर्मक्षेत्रे कुरुक्षेत्रे समवेता युयुत्सवः ।
मामकाः पाण्डवाश्चैव किमकुर्वत सञ्जय ॥ १-१ ॥

*सञ्जय उवाच –*

दृष्ट्वा तु पाण्डवानीकं व्यूढं दुर्योधनस्तदा ।
आचार्यमुपसङ्गम्य राजा वचनमब्रवीत् ॥ १-२ ॥
पश्यैतां पाण्डुपुत्राणामाचार्य महतीं चमूम् ।
व्यूढां द्रुपदपुत्रेण तव शिष्येण धीमता ॥ १-३ ॥

### द्वितीयोऽध्यायः - साङ्ख्ययोगः

### तृतीयोऽध्यायः - कर्मयोगः

### चतुर्थोऽध्यायः - ज्ञानकर्मसंन्यासयोगः

### पञ्चमोऽध्यायः - संन्यासयोगः

### षष्ठोऽध्यायः - ध्यानयोगः

### सप्तमोऽध्यायः - ज्ञानविज्ञानयोगः

### अष्टमोऽध्यायः - अक्षरब्रह्मयोगः

### नवमोऽध्यायः - राजविद्याराजगुह्ययोगः

### दशमोऽध्यायः - विभूतियोगः

### एकादशोऽध्यायः - विश्वरूपदर्शनयोगः

### द्वादशोऽध्यायः - भक्तियोगः

### त्रयोदशोऽध्यायः - क्षेत्रक्षेत्रज्ञविभागयोगः

### चतुर्दशोऽध्यायः - गुणत्रयविभागयोगः

### पञ्चदशोऽध्यायः - पुरुषोत्तमयोगः

### षोडशोऽध्यायः - दैवासुरसम्पद्विभागयोगः

### सप्तदशोऽध्यायः - श्रद्धात्रयविभागयोगः

### अष्टादशोऽध्यायः - मोक्षसंन्यासयोगः

—ॐ— ध्यानम् —ॐ— dhyānam —ॐ—

# ॐ INVOCATIONS

ॐ श्री परमात्मने नमः
— om śrī paramātmane namaḥ —
**[Om—I bow down to the Supreme-Energy, Supreme-Being]**

**त्वमेव माता च पिता त्वमेव । त्वमेव बंधुश्च सखा त्वमेव ।**
tvameva mātā ca pitā tvameva , tvameva baṁdhuśca sakhā tvameva ,
**त्वमेव विद्या द्रविणं त्वमेव । त्वमेव सर्वं मम देवदेव ॥**
tvameva vidyā draviṇaṁ tvameva , tvameva sarvaṁ mama devadeva .

**Thou art my mother and my father, Thou alone my kin, kith, friend; Thou alone my wisdom, knowledge, wealth; Thou alone—O God of gods—my all, and everything!**

—ॐ—

**शान्ताकारं भुजगशयनं पद्मनाभं सुरेशं । विश्वाधारं गगनसदृशं मेघवर्णं शुभाङ्गम् ।**
śāntākāraṁ bhujagaśayanaṁ padmanābhaṁ sureśaṁ
viśvādhāraṁ gaganasadṛśaṁ meghavarṇaṁ śubhāṅgam ,
**लक्ष्मीकान्तं कमलनयनं योगिभिर्ध्यानगम्यं । वन्दे विष्णुं भवभयहरं सर्वलोकैकनाथम् ॥**
lakṣmīkāntaṁ kamalanayanaṁ yogibhirdhyānagamyaṁ
vande viṣṇuṁ bhavabhayaharaṁ sarvalokaikanātham .

**I venerate Shri Vishnu—of a serene appearance who slumbers upon the serpent *Shesha-Nāga*, from whose navel has sprung the lotus of creation, who presides over as the God of gods, who is the substratum of the universe, boundless and infinite like the sky. Of a dark hue like the clouds, of a form radiating everlasting auspiciousness, with eyes beautiful like lotus petals, who is the beloved of Devī Lakshmī, who is reachable only through devotional meditation by Yogīs, who removes all fears of worldly existence—upon Him, Vishnu, the One Great Lord of all the worlds, I meditate.**

—ॐ—

**यं ब्रह्मा वरुणेन्द्ररुद्रमरुतः स्तुन्वन्ति दिव्यैः स्तवैः**
yaṁ brahmā varuṇendrarudramarutaḥ stunvanti divyaiḥ stavaiḥ
**वेदैः साङ्गपदक्रमोपनिषदैर्गायन्ति यं सामगाः ।**
vedaiḥ sāṅgapadakramopaniṣadairgāyanti yaṁ sāmagāḥ ,
**ध्यानावस्थिततद्गतेन मनसा पश्यन्ति यं योगिनो**
dhyānāvasthitatadgatena manasā paśyanti yaṁ yogino
**यस्यान्तं न विदुः सुरासुरगणा देवाय तस्मै नमः ॥**
yasyāntaṁ na viduḥ surāsuragaṇā devāya tasmai namaḥ .

Unto That Supreme—whom Brahammā, Varuna, Indra, Rudra and the Mārutas praise with excellent holy hymns; who is versified throughout the Vedas and Upanishads by the chanters of Sāma; who—in perfect meditations deep—the yogis see within their own minds while absorbed in "That-One"; whose beginning and end, even gods and demi-gods never know of—unto That Supreme-Being, I offer my many venerations.

ॐ ॐ ॐ ॐ ॐ ॐ ॐ ॐ ॐ ॐ ॐ ॐ ॐ ॐ ॐ ॐ ॐ ॐ

—ॐ— स्तुतिः —ॐ— stutiḥ —ॐ—

—ॐ—ॐ—ॐ—ॐ—ॐ—ॐ—

**<u>VENERATIONS</u>**

—ॐ—

पार्थाय प्रतिबोधितां भगवता नारायणेन स्वयम्
pārthāya pratibodhitāṁ bhagavatā nārāyaṇena svayam
व्यासेनग्रथितां पुराणमुनिना मध्ये महाभारते ।
vyāsenagrathitāṁ purāṇamuninā madhye mahābhārate ,
अद्वैतामृतवर्षिणीं भगवतीमष्टादशाध्यायिनीम्
advaitāmṛtavarṣiṇīṁ bhagavatīmaṣṭādaśādhyāyinīm
अम्ब त्वामनुसन्दधामि भगवद्गीते भवेद्वेषिणीम् ॥
amba tvāmanusandadhāmi bhagavadgīte bhavedveṣiṇīm .

O Thou Bhagavad-Gītā—with whom Pārtha was enlightened by the Lord Nārāyana himself; who was integrated into the Mahābhārata by the ancient sage Vyāsa; O Thou blessed Mother—who with her eighteen Cantos shower humanity with the nectar of Advaita; O Thou destroyer of rebirths, upon Thee—O Bhagavad-Gītā, O loving Mother—I meditate.

—ॐ—

नमोऽस्तु ते व्यास विशालबुद्धे फुल्लारविन्दायतपत्रनेत्र ।
namo'stu te vyāsa viśālabuddhe phullāravindāyatapatranetra ,
येन त्वया भारततैलपूर्णः प्रज्वालितो ज्ञानमयः प्रदीपः ॥
yena tvayā bhāratatailapūrṇaḥ prajvālito jñānamayaḥ pradīpaḥ .

Salutations to Thee O Vyāsa—of a mighty intellect and with eyes large like the petals of a full-blossomed lotus; by whom has been forever lit in this world the Lamp-of-Wisdom, filled with the oil in the form of the great epic: Mahābhārata.

— ॐ —

प्रपन्नपारिजाताय तोत्रवेत्रैकपाणये ।
prapannapārijātāya totravetraikapāṇaye ,
ज्ञानमुद्राय कृष्णाय गीतामृतदुहे नमः ॥
jñānamudrāya kṛṣṇāya gītāmṛtaduhe namaḥ .

**He—who is the wish-granting tree of the suppliant—in whose one hand is held the rope for cow and with the other hand who holds the Yogic posture of *Jnana*—who is the milcher of the nectar known as Gītā—unto Him, Krishna, my repeated venerations.**

— ॐ —

सर्वोपनिषदो गावो दोग्धा गोपालनन्दनः ।
sarvopaniṣado gāvo dogdhā gopālanandanaḥ ,
पार्थो वत्सः सुधीर्भोक्ता दुग्धं गीतामृतं महत् ॥
pārtho vatsaḥ sudhīrbhoktā dugdhaṁ gītāmṛtaṁ mahat .

**All the Upanishads are the cows; the milcher is the joy of cowherds, Krishna; Pārtha is the calf; the man of purified understanding is the partaker; and the milk is verily the supreme nectar known as Gītā.**

— ॐ —

वसुदेवसुतं देवं कंसचाणूरमर्दनम् ।
vasudevasutaṁ devaṁ kaṁsacāṇūramardanam ,
देवकीपरमानन्दं कृष्णं वन्दे जगद्गुरुम् ॥
devakīparamānandaṁ kṛṣṇaṁ vande jagadgurum .

**I worship the charioteer, the Lord-God, the destroyer of Kamsa and Chānura, the supreme joy of Devakī, the son of Vāsudeva—Shri Krishna, the Universal Guru.**

— ॐ —

भीष्मद्रोणतटा जयद्रथजला गान्धारनीलोत्पला
bhīṣmadroṇataṭā jayadrathajalā gāndhāranīlotpalā
शल्यग्राहवती कृपेण वहनी कर्णेन वेलाकुला ।
śalyagrāhavatī kṛpeṇa vahanī karṇena velākulā ,
अश्वत्थामविकर्णघोरमकरा दुर्योधनावर्तिनी
aśvatthāmavikarṇaghoramakarā duryodhanāvartinī
सोत्तीर्णा खलु पाण्डवैरणनदी कैवर्तकः केशवः ॥
sottīrṇā khalu pāṇḍavairaṇanadī kaivartakaḥ keśavaḥ .

**That terrible battle-river—which had Bhīṣma and Droṇa as its two banks, and Jayadrathaja as its waters; which had the king of Gāndhāra as its blue lotus, and Śalya as its shark; whose currents and billows were Kṛipā and Karṇa; which had Aśvatthāmā and Vikarṇa as its terrible alligators; and of which Duryodhana was the deadly whirlpool—that ferocious river could be forded by the Pāṇḍavas only because they had Keśava as their helmsman.**

— ॐ —

पाराशर्यवचः सरोजममलं गीतार्थगन्धोत्कटं
pārāśaryavacaḥ sarojamamalaṁ gītārthagandhotkaṭaṁ
नानाख्यानककेसरं हरिकथासम्बोधनाबोधितम्।
nānākhyānakakesaraṁ harikathāsambodhanābodhitam ।
लोके सज्जनषट्पदैरहरहः पेपीयमानं मुदा
loke sajjanaṣaṭpadairaharahaḥ pepīyamānaṁ mudā
भूयाद्भारतपङ्कजं कलिमलप्रध्वंसिनः श्रेयसे ॥
bhūyādbhāratapaṅkajaṁ kalimalapradhvaṁsinaḥ śreyase .

**May this Lotus called Mahābhārata—which was born on the lake of the words of Vyāsa—which is perfumed with the fragrance of the Purport-of-Gītā—which has its innumerous stories as the pollen—which became fully bloomed through the discourses of Hari—which is the destroyer of the sins of the Kali-Yuga—which is everyday partaken joyously by the bees in the shape of good people of the world—may it bestow all goodness upon us.**

— ॐ —

मूकं करोति वाचालं पङ्गुं लङ्घयते गिरिम् ।
mūkaṁ karoti vācālaṁ paṅguṁ laṅghayate girim ,
यत्कृपा तमहं वन्दे परमानन्दमाधवम् ॥
yatkṛpā tamahaṁ vande paramānandamādhavam .

**I salute the Supreme-Being of the nature of supreme bliss, by whose very grace the dumb become eloquent and the cripples step across mountains.**

— ॐ —

ॐ पूर्णमदः पूर्णमिदं पूर्णात् पूर्णमुदच्यते ।
om pūrṇamadaḥ pūrṇamidaṁ pūrṇāt pūrṇamudacyate ,
पूर्णस्य पूर्णमादाय पूर्णमेवावशिष्यते ।
pūrṇasya pūrṇamādāya pūrṇamevāvaśiṣyate ,
ॐ शान्तिः शान्तिः शान्तिः ॥
om śāntiḥ śāntiḥ śāntiḥ .

**Om—That One (the unmanifest Brahma)—is infinite, complete, Entire; this (the manifest universe) is entire; And from That One fullness has emerged this entire universe here; And even when this entirety here is taken out of that One-Entire, It still abides complete in all Its entireness! Om, peace—let there be tranquility all around me!**

— ॐ — ॐ — ॐ — ॐ — ॐ — ॐ — ॐ — ॐ — ॐ —

ॐ ॐ ॐ ॐ ॐ ॐ ॐ ॐ ॐ ॐ ॐ ॐ ॐ ॐ ॐ ॐ ॐ ॐ

# ॐ The Gītā-Journey Thus Far

— ॐ तत सत ॐ —

The Bhagavad-Gītā, often referred to as the "Song of God," is a spiritual and philosophical dialogue nestled within the Indian epic Mahābhārata. It unfolds on the battlefield of Kurukṣetra, where the warrior-prince Arjuna, torn by moral dilemmas and inner conflict, turns to his charioteer—none other than the Lord-God Bhagwāna Shri Krishna—for guidance. What follows is a timeless conversation that delves into the deepest questions of life, duty, self-realization, and the nature of the cosmos and Self.

Outwardly, it might appear to be a call to arms, but the Bhagavad-Gitā is a profound manual for living life—with wisdom, purpose, and spiritual integrity.

— ॐ —

The Gitā journey begins in **Chapter 1:** Arjuna Viṣāda Yoga, where Arjuna is overcome with sorrow and confusion upon seeing his relatives, teachers, and friends arrayed on both sides of the battlefield. Paralyzed by moral anguish, he puts down his bow, unable to fight. This sets the stage for Krishna's teachings.

In **Chapter 2:** Sāṅkhya Yoga, Krishna initiates Arjuna into the philosophy of the soul (Ātmā), explaining its immortality and the impermanence of the body. He introduces the ideas of equanimity (abiding as a witness) and action for dharma's sake (karma-yoga) as essential for spiritual progress.

— ॐ —

**Chapters 3 to 6** develop these foundational concepts:

- **Chapter 3, Karma Yoga,** explores the path of selfless action as a means to transcend bondage.
- **Chapter 4, Jñāna Karma Sannyāsa Yoga,** combines wisdom and action, emphasizing that right understanding purifies action.
- **Chapter 5, Karma Sannyāsa Yoga,** contrasts renunciation and disciplined action, ultimately showing their harmony.
- **Chapter 6, Dhyāna Yoga,** introduces meditation as the means to mastery of the mind and union with the Self.

With **Chapter 7, Jñāna-Vijñāna Yoga,** the tone deepens. Krishna begins to reveal his divine nature, moving from philosophical abstraction to theistic clarity. He shows how knowledge (jñāna) coupled with realization (vijñāna) leads to true devotion.

— ॐ —

**Chapters 8 to 11** continue to elevate Arjuna's vision:

- **Chapter 8, Akṣara Brahma Yoga,** discusses the eternal Braham and the soul's journey after death.
- **Chapter 9, Rāja-Vidyā Rāja-Guhya Yoga,** unveils the king of sciences—the supreme secret: that loving devotion to Krishna is the highest path.
- **Chapter 10, Vibhūti Yoga,** elaborates on Krishna's divine manifestations in the world.
- **Chapter 11, Viśvarūpa Darśana Yoga,** reaches a climax as Krishna grants Arjuna the divine eye to behold his cosmic form, a staggering revelation of the universal Lord beyond all imagination.

— ॐ —

Now, in **Chapter 12, Bhakti Yoga,** the Gītā turns its focus fully on bhakti—the path of loving devotion.

Arjuna, awed by the vision of the Divine, asks whether worshiping the formless Braham or the personal God is superior. Krishna answers with clarity and compassion, emphasizing that sincere devotion to a personal God, guided by humility, love, and surrender, leads swiftly to liberation. He outlines the qualities of true devotee—one who is dear to Him—not by external rituals, but by his inner purity, equanimity, and selfless love.

— ॐ —

As the Gītā progresses from here on, **Chapters 13 to 18** will turn to deeper philosophical analysis. These final chapters revisit key ideas—dissecting the distinction between the field (kṣetra) and the knower (kṣetrajña), exploring the interplay of the three guṇas (modes of nature), the nature of faith, the classification of actions, and ultimately, the synthesis of all paths. The journey culminates in a comprehensive vision of the spiritual life—rooted in knowledge, sustained by action, and perfected in devotion.

Meanwhile, **Chapter 12** stands as a luminous centerpoint in the Gītā, bridging the majesty of divine revelation with the intimacy of heartfelt devotion—a reminder that the highest truth is not just to be known, but to be directly realized: with love.

# ॐ CHAPTER TWELVE, A BIRD'S-EYE VIEW

— ॐ तत सत ॐ —

## BHAKTI YOGA

In Chapter 12 of the Bhagavad-Gītā, titled Bhakti Yoga—"The Path of Devotion"—Lord Krishna delivers one of the most accessible and heart-centered teachings in the entire text. Having revealed His cosmic form in Chapter 11 and with Arjuna whelmed with awe, Krishna now turns to a gentler, more intimate path: Devotion. This chapter distills the essence of the Gītā's message into a simple, profound truth—God is not merely to be known, but to be loved.

The chapter begins with a question from Arjuna that many spiritual seekers wrestle with: Is it better to worship the formless, unmanifest Absolute (nirguṇa brahman), or to adore the personal God with form (saguṇa īśvara)? Krishna's answer is clear and compassionate: while both paths are valid, the path of personal devotion is more natural and accessible for most.

From there the chapter unfolds as a step-by-step guide to cultivating devotion. It recognizes the diversity of human temperament and lays out a compassionate ladder of spiritual practice—from pure devotion to disciplined meditation, selfless action, and even detachment from the fruits of work. As it progresses, Krishna describes the qualities of a true devotee, one who is dear to Him—not for outward rituals, but for their inner grace: humility, forgiveness, compassion, and unwavering equanimity.

Some consider the Chapter 12 to be the heart of the Gītā—as if it's the Gītā's heart speaking to ours—but not so much the Jñāni; they find chapter 13, 15, etc., to be more sublime. In fact it is a tough call—for the entirety of Gitā is most beautiful and sublime.

— ॐ —

## BHAKTI YOGA: A VERSE-BY-VERSE OVERVIEW

After witnessing the awe-inspiring cosmic form of Krishna in Chapter 11, Arjuna now seeks to understand a subtler truth: What is the best way to approach the Divine—through devotion to the personal God or contemplation of the impersonal Absolute?

*Verse 1 depicts this question of Arjuna's:*

Arjuna asks: Who is the better yogi—those who worship You with form (saguṇa) or those who meditate on the formless Absolute (nirguṇa)?

This is a classic dilemma for spiritual seekers: Bhakti (devotion) vs. Jñāna (knowledge of the formless).

*Verses 2–3, Krishna's Immediate Response:*

Krishna affirms: Those who fix their minds on Me with supreme faith and devotion are considered the most perfect in yoga.

But He also praises those who meditate on the unmanifest—steadfast and self-restrained—but then again...

*Verse 4–5, The Difficulty of the Formless Path:*

Krishna compassionately admits: The path of meditating on the unmanifest is difficult and abstract. It demands intense self-discipline and detachment, which can be too challenging for embodied beings.

*Verses 6–7, The Power of Personal Devotion:*

Those who worship Him with mind and heart, surrendering all actions to Him, are lovingly protected. Krishna promises to lift them from the ocean of saṁsāra (birth and death).

This is a deeply reassuring verse—God is not a distant ideal, but a Savior who looks-out for those who reach-out to Him.

*Verse 8, Fix Your Mind on Me:*

Krishna begins with the highest recommendation: "Just fix your mind and intellect on Me alone—then you will live in Me."

This is the ideal bhakti—complete absorption in God.

*Verse 9, If You Can't Do That... Practice:*

If full mental absorption is too difficult, then abhyāsa—spiritual practice—is advised. Practice focusing on God daily, gradually deepening your devotion.

*Verse 10, If Practice Is Too Hard... Act for Me:*

Still too hard? Then engage in selfless action—perform duties with the intention of pleasing God. This is karma yoga infused with bhakti.

*Verse 11, If Even That Feels Distant... Renounce the Results:*

If even acting for God feels abstract, then simply renounce the fruits of action. Let go of attachment to outcomes. This itself leads to peace.

This progressive descent shows Krishna's compassion—He meets us where we are.

*Verse 12, Why Devotion is Supreme:*

Krishna ranks the approaches: knowledge is greater than mere practice, meditation greater than knowledge, but best of all is renunciation of the fruits of action—because it brings immediate peace.

This verse subtly weaves together all yogic paths, culminating in the peace of bhakti.

*Verses 13–14, Qualities of the True Devotee (Part 1):*

Here begins a beautiful list: A true devotee is free from hatred, is friendly and compassionate, without ego or possessiveness, content and steady, self-controlled, and mindfully surrendered to God.

*Verses 15–16, Qualities of the True Devotee (Part 2):*

Such a person causes no fear or disturbance to others and remains unmoved by external conditions—free from joy, envy, fear, and anxiety. Detached from possessions, pure, skillful, and non-demanding.

These verses reflect a fully matured heart—soft, resilient, and inwardly free.

*Verses 17–18, Qualities of the True Devotee (Part 3):*

A true devotee is indifferent to praise and blame, silent, content with whatever comes, free from dualities, and full of love. Such a one is balanced in honor and dishonor, treating friend and foe alike.

This is the culmination of inner equanimity—the fruit of true bhakti.

*Verse 19, Summary:*

Whoever lives with this inner spirit of devotion and abides in love, that devotee is most dear to Me.

Krishna is not impressed by outer rituals or renunciation—but by the quiet humility and unwavering love of the devotee.

*Verse 20, Final Blessing:*

Those who follow this path of sacred devotion, with deep faith and a heart full of surrender, are exceedingly dear to Me.

This final verse is like a garland, tying together all the qualities previously described. It assures us that bhakti is not about perfection, but about sincerity.

— ॐ —

Chapter 12 is a tender and inclusive teaching. It honors both the path of knowledge and the path of devotion but emphasizes that the heart's love, expressed through humility, equanimity, and surrender, is the highest and most accessible way to become united with the Divine.

Whether we are intellectuals, meditators, workers, or simple seekers of peace, Krishna makes room for us all—guiding each of us with patience, offering stepping stones, and assuring us: "If you walk toward Me with love—I, the Lord-God, will in turn receive you with open arms."

— ॐ भवबन्धविमोचकाय नमः ॐ —

The Sermon of Bhagwâna Shri Krishna

O mortal, hear to the Lord's gentle summons
"Place thy mind in Me," He says, as He bends to lift human heart,
"Fix thy thought-and-knowing both—in Me, and never part."
This is no cold decree of some Deity, no distant edict stern—
But invitation clothed in gold, with love and reason fused as one.

No thorny law, no iron gate—but open hands outspread,
A call to cease the restless flight and rest thy weary head.
"मय्येव"Mayi eva"—in Me alone"—thy heart must weave its flame:
- In **Krishna**, the King of kings, Soul of souls,
Let the sky, let all thoughts—converge into just that One-Name कृष्ण

It's A Simple Command—Yet Stays Unheeded, Unheard

Fix thy mind on Me, Bhagwana Shri Krishna says,
Not on the world,
—Not this, that, I, me, mine, here, there, other —
But always on the Eternal-Flame.
And then—
Thou too shalt become verily that Flame.
Have no doubts—know this with full certainty.

Hear Ye Mortal:

You were meant to be flame.
You chose smoke.
You were meant to be the ocean.
You chase puddles.
You were meant to be the Self.
You choose the shadow.
And yet — that patient Âtmâ, still waits within.
O come on man, wake up already.

ॐ ॐ ॐ ॐ ॐ ॐ ॐ ॐ ॐ ॐ ॐ ॐ ॐ ॐ ॐ ॐ ॐ ॐ

## द्वादशोऽध्यायः - भक्तियोगः
## dvādaśo'dhyāyaḥ - bhaktiyogaḥ
## :: Canto – XII ::
## - The Path of Bhakti -

ॐ ॐ ॐ ॐ ॐ ॐ ॐ ॐ ॐ ॐ ॐ ॐ ॐ ॐ ॐ ॐ ॐ ॐ

## ॐ गीता श्लोकः १२.१ – GĪTĀ VERSE 12.1

ॐ श्रीमद्भगवद्गीतासूपनिषत्सु ब्रह्मविद्यायां योगशास्त्रे श्रीकृष्णार्जुनसंवादे
om śrīmadbhagavadgītāsūpaniṣatsu brahmavidyāyāṁ yogaśāstre śrīkṛṣṇārjunasaṁvāde
भक्तियोगो नाम द्वादशोऽध्यायः श्लोकः १
bhaktiyogo nāma dvādaśo'dhyāyaḥ ślokaḥ 1

— ॐ —

*अर्जुन उवाच --*
*arjuna uvāca --*

**एवं सततयुक्ता ये भक्तास्त्वां पर्युपासते ।**
**evaṁ satatayuktā ye bhaktāstvāṁ paryupāsate**
**ये चाप्यक्षरमव्यक्तं तेषां के योगवित्तमाः ॥ १२-१ ॥**
**ye cāpyakṣaramavyaktaṁ teṣāṁ ke yogavittamāḥ** (12-1)

***Arjuna said:* "Of devotees who worship you in the manner you just spoke of—with having a manifest form, and those who worship you as the Imperishable-Absolute of unmanifest form—of those two, who is to be considered better versed in Yoga?" (12.1)**

*—: Word-by-Word :—*

**अर्जुन उवाच** arjuna uvāca – Arjuna said; **एवं** evaṁ – thus; **सतत-युक्ताः** satata-yuktāḥ – constantly engaged; **ये** ye – those who; **भक्ताः** bhaktāḥ – are devotees; **त्वाम्** tvāṁ – to you; **पर्युपासते** paryupāsate – worship; **ये** ye – those who; **च** ca – and; **अपि** api – also; **अक्षरम्** akṣaram – the imperishable; **अव्यक्तम्** avyaktaṁ – the unmanifest; **तेषां** teṣāṁ – of them; **के** ke – who; **योग-वित्तमाः** yogavittamāḥ – are the most knowledgeable in yoga.

*—: Understanding The Verse :—*

— ॐ श्रीकृष्णाय नमः ॐ —

Here Arjuna—as any earnest seeker of truth will do—humbly approaches Bhagwāna Shri Krishna with a question that naturally arises in the heart of those treading the path of Yoga.

Arjuna has just heard Shri Krishna expound upon various modes of spiritual practice and devotion—particularly the glories of unwavering bhakti delineated at the end of the eleventh chapter—

and now Arjuna seeks clarity regarding the relative excellence of the two celebrated paths.

— ॐ योगिनां पतये नमः ॐ —

On the one side stands the path of devotion unto the Creator who has become manifest in name and form—i.e., worship directed toward the personal form of the Divine, resplendent with auspicious qualities, accessible to the heart and senses of the devotee;

and on the other stands the arduous path of contemplation upon the formless, unmanifest imperishable Absolute—Braham, who is beyond name, form, attributes, grasped only by the keen intellect and purified mind.

Now which path is better?

— ॐ यज्ञेश्वराय नमः ॐ —

Arjuna's inquiry reflects the perennial spiritual tension between saguna (with attributes) and nirguna (without attributes) modalities of bhakti;

and Arjuna's question impels Shri Krishna to illuminate the intrinsic merits of both—guiding not only Arjuna but all earnest aspirants toward the path most conducive to their highest welfare.

## *—: Key Sanskrit Terms :—*

— ॐ तत सत ॐ —

Let us linger with the Sanskrit as with a disciple's soft question to a master: "एवं सततयुक्ता ये भक्तास्त्वां पर्युपासते । ये चाप्यक्षरमव्यक्तं तेषां के योगवित्तमाः ॥ Who is better—those who worship You with devotion, or those who worship the imperishable, the unmanifest?" Each syllable is yearning, reaching toward certainty.

Now let us unfold the inner meaning of the verse:

— ॐ —

एवं सततयुक्ताः (evaṁ satatayuktāḥ):

Here, सततयुक्ताः (satatayuktāḥ) suggests a soul ever-joined, ever-engaged in divine contemplation without cessation.

- सतत satata — continuous, and "
- युक्ताः yukta — yoked, united, steadfast.

It evokes the image of a being whose consciousness is not merely intermittently religious but whose entire existence is a flow of unbroken remembrance (स्मरण smaraṇa) and offering (अर्पण arpana).

It speaks not merely of outer actions but of a soul internally, immovably riveted to the Divine.

— ॐ —

भक्ताः (bhaktāḥ):

The term भक्ताः (bhaktāḥ) — devotees — is rich with tenderness and profound surrender. Bhakti is not mere emotional sentiment;

it is the soul's recognition of its eternal belonging (नित्य सम्बंध nitya-sambandha) to the Supreme.

A bhakta is one whose individuality has melted into the divine beloved, where love (प्रेम prema) is not a transaction but the very texture of existence.

— ॐ —

त्वाम् पर्युपासते (tvām paryupāsate):

- परोपासन (paryupāsana) denotes not just worship but a surrounding, an immersion.

It is worship wherein the worshipper revolve around—mentally and existentially —the worshipped, offering all movements of body, mind, and breath.

- त्वाम् पर्युपासते tvām paryupāsate conveys an adoration wherein the Supreme Lord is approached as the nearest and the dearest, worshipped through surrender of selfhood.

— ॐ —

अक्षरम् अव्यक्तम् (akṣaram avyaktam):

- अक्षरम् (akṣaram) — the Imperishable — bespeaks the unchanging Reality that lies beyond the mutabilities of name and form.

It is the unwithering foundation upon which all evanescent phenomena make their fleeting dance.

- अव्यक्तम् (avyaktam) — the Unmanifest — describes that which cannot be grasped by the senses or shaped by thought;

it stands aloof from attributes and imagery, a presence in negation, a fullness behind veils.

— ॐ —

योगवित्तमाः (yogavittamāḥ):

- वित्तमाः (vittamāḥ) — best knowers, most skillful.

Here, those who are योगवित yogavit — knowers of Yoga — are those who have not merely read or theorized, but who have realized Yoga — the union of self and Supreme.

It is not a mechanical knowledge but a wisdom born from tasting the oneness of Being.

The term suggests mastery not in outer artifice but in the subtle, inward alchemy of spiritual consummation.

### —: *In Brief* :—

— ॐ श्रीकृष्णाय नमः ॐ —

Arjuna's question arises from a profound spiritual concern, not born of idle curiosity but of a deep longing to comprehend the nature of ultimate human attainment.

By referring to the devotees who worship "एवं evam"—in the manner previously described—Arjuna recalls the path of steadfast, exclusive devotion extolled by Shri Krishna at the conclusion of the eleventh chapter, where the devotee surrenders all actions, fixing the mind and heart solely upon the Lord.

Yet Arjuna, ever thoughtful, recognizes that another path is known to the wise: the arduous pursuit of the formless Braham, the imperishable, unmanifest Reality, beyond all sensory grasp, beyond all conceptualization.

— ॐ श्रीरामाय नमः ॐ —

The use of the word त्वाम् tvām (to You) is significant.

Though uttered in the immediate context of Bhagwāna Shri Krishna, Arjuna's words transcend the historical moment and encompass the Supreme Lord in all His divine manifestations, whether as the Avatāras that descend age after age or as the eternally resplendent form dwelling in His transcendental abode.

The heart of the personalist devotee clings to this form with love, directing all senses, thoughts, and feelings toward it in a spirit of selfless surrender.

By contrast अव्यक्तम् अक्षरम् avyaktam akṣaram points unmistakably to the attributeless Braham, the unmanifest Absolute—pure Existence, Consciousness, and Bliss.

Though the terms अव्यक्त avyakta and अक्षर akṣara can sometimes refer to the subtle aspect of the individual self (jīvātman), Arjuna's intention here is unmistakably toward the supreme, transcendent Braham, the ultimate ground of all being.

— ॐ वनवासप्रियाय नमः ॐ —

In his heart, Arjuna discerns the nobility of both paths, yet he yearns to know which path leads more surely to perfect union with the Divine.

Arjuna's question reveals the underlying human concern: how best to bridge the chasm between the finite and the Infinite, the temporal and the Eternal.

In response, Shri Krishna will graciously reveal that while both paths are lofty, the path of devotion to the manifest Lord, undertaken with a heart full of love and single-minded surrender, is both more accessible and more efficacious for embodied beings who dwell in a world of name and form.

— ॐ तपस्विने नमः ॐ —

Arjuna's question paves the way for one of the most beautiful teachings of the Bhagavad-Gītā, where Shri Krishna extols the supreme excellence of bhakti as the surest and most intimate means of attaining the Highest.

See how the Gītā gently continues leading us into the inner sanctum of divine love—preparing the ground for more sublime instructions that keep flowing verse after verse.

— ॐ तत सत ॐ —

Before moving on, let us once more bow in deep reverence before this sacred verse of the Bhagavad-Gītā, an eternal beacon of wisdom that ceaselessly illumines the path of seekers. Engage with its form—inscribe it with your own hand, let your heart dwell upon its meaning, and raise your voice in its chanting—for within these syllables echoes the undying proclamation delivered millennia ago on the battlefield of Kurukshetra. These words, transmitted unchanged across the unbroken chain of generations, form a living bridge, linking us to that sanctified era when Bhagwāna Shri Krishna Himself walked this earth and bestowed this divine teaching. Through the luminous vibration of these sacred Sanskrit sounds, we are drawn nearer to His timeless presence, touching the very heartbeat of the Eternal.

— ॐ —

*अर्जुन उवाच --*
*arjuna uvāca --*

**एवं सततयुक्ता ये भक्तास्त्वां पर्युपासते ।**
**evaṁ satatayuktā ye bhaktāstvāṁ paryupāsate**
**ये चाप्यक्षरमव्यक्तं तेषां के योगवित्तमाः ॥१२-१॥**
**ye cāpyakṣaramavyaktaṁ teṣāṁ ke yogavittamāḥ (12-1)**

— ॐ —

अर्जुन उवाच --
arjuna uvāca --

एवं सततयुक्ता ये भक्तास्त्वां पर्युपासते ।
evaṁ satatayuktā ye bhaktāstvāṁ paryupāsate
ये चाप्यक्षरमव्यक्तं तेषां के योगवित्तमाः ॥१२-१॥
ye cāpyakṣaramavyaktaṁ teṣāṁ ke yogavittamāḥ (12-1)

ॐ तत्सदिति श्रीमद्भगवद्गीतासूपनिषत्सु ब्रह्मविद्यायां योगशास्त्रे श्रीकृष्णार्जुनसंवादे
om tatsaditi śrīmadbhagavadgītāsūpaniṣatsu brahmavidyāyāṁ yogaśāstre śrīkṛṣṇārjunasaṁvāde
भक्तियोगो नाम द्वादशोऽध्यायः श्लोकः १
bhaktiyogo nāma dvādaśo'dhyāyaḥ ślokaḥ 1

**Om-Tat-Sat—Om (Braham) is the sole Reality. In the Yogic Scripture on the Science-of-Braham, the Shrimada-Bhāgvada-Gītā Upanishad, we hereby conclude Shloka 1 of the Dialogue between Shrī Krishna and Arjuna entitled Bhakti-Yoga, Canto XII.**

— ॐ श्रीकेशवाय नमः ॐ —

The Knotted Heart of the Seeker

O my wavering mind, torn in twain —
Why dost thou linger in twilight's mist, uncertain?
Drawn by love's form, yet haunted by the void?
To whom shall I surrender — the Seen or the Unseen?

One path sings with sweetness — form divine, resplendent,
The other is silence — vast, formless, bare of hue & shape,
My mind wavers, stretched between two poles,
Craving nearness to the with-form God—
Yet also pulled to the Fathomless Depth.
My heart is in confusion, seeking the face of Eternal
What really leads truly to He — the True God, the ever-free?

The Manifest Leads to the Unmanifest

O child of eternity, hear the wisdom of the great Rishis:
The Form is but the window to the Formless Reality.
Approach the Lord with love — let thy heart be light,
Over time, He shall draw thee beyond all sounds and sights.

One who loves Him as Krishna, also knows Him as the formless Braham —
For He is both: the Wave and the Boundless Sea.
Worship the Seen, and for sure—one day He shall reveal the Unseen,
Serve with heart and song—and one day be lifted beyond all dualities.
Tat-Tvam-Asi — O soul, thou art That,
So let Krishna lead thee Home — to the shoreless sea of eternal Bliss.

But Do Not Stay Frozen In Doubt

Either which way, proceed on thy quest—thou hast tarried enough,
Let not thy doubts suspend thee in an uncertainty sea of mist,
Go ahead, reach out for the hand of Krishna—
let Him Himself lead thee out.

## ॐ गीता श्लोकः १२.२ – GĪTĀ VERSE 12.2

ॐ श्रीमद्भगवद्गीतासूपनिषत्सु ब्रह्मविद्यायां योगशास्त्रे श्रीकृष्णार्जुनसंवादे
om śrīmadbhagavadgītāsūpaniṣatsu brahmavidyāyāṁ yogaśāstre śrīkṛṣṇārjunasaṁvāde
भक्तियोगो नाम द्वादशोऽध्यायः श्लोकः २
bhaktiyogo nāma dvādaśo'dhyāyaḥ ślokaḥ 2

— ॐ —

*श्रीभगवानुवाच --*
*śrībhagavānuvāca --*

**मय्यावेश्य मनो ये मां नित्ययुक्ता उपासते ।**
**mayyāveśya mano ye māṁ nityayuktā upāsate**
**श्रद्धया परयोपेताः ते मे युक्ततमा मताः** ॥१२-२॥
**śraddhayā parayopetāḥ te me yuktatamā matāḥ** (12-2)

***Shri Bhagwāna said:* "Ever devoted and endowed with supreme faith, those who fix their minds upon Me as the Lord-God of manifest form, and worship thusly—them I deem to be higher.** (12.2)

*—: Word-by-Word :—*

**श्रीभगवानुवाच** śrībhagavān uvāca – the Blessed Lord said; **मयि** mayi – in me; **आवेश्य** āveśya – fixing; **मनः** manaḥ – the mind; **ये** ye – those who; **माम्** mām – me; **नित्य-युक्ताः** nitya-yuktāḥ – ever steadfast; **उपासते** upāsate – worship; **श्रद्धया** śraddhayā – with faith; **परयोपेताः** paraya-upetāḥ – endowed with supreme; **ते** te – they; **मे** me – by me; **युक्ततमाः** yuktatamāḥ – the most united (in yoga); **मताः** matāḥ – are considered.

***—: Understanding The Verse :—***

— ॐ श्रीकृष्णाय नमः ॐ —

In gracious reply to Arjuna's earnest inquiry, Bhagwāna Shri Krishna now reveals the excellence of those devotees whose hearts are wholly fixed upon Him. The Lord declares that those who worship Him with unwavering devotion, their minds absorbed in His divine form, and who are endowed with supreme faith, are to be regarded as the highest among Yogis.

This verse extols the way of Bhakti—the yoga of loving devotion—as surpassing the arduous contemplative path directed toward the formless Absolute.

— ॐ यतिरूपाय नमः ॐ —

Shri Krishna emphasizes that it is not mere intellectual understanding nor the dry austerity of renunciation that wins the

Lord's favor, but rather the loving, steadfast surrender of one's entire being to Him.

The verse also subtly anticipates the need to clarify the position of the jñāni, the knower of Braham, which Shri Krishna will address in the later verses.

The stage is now set for a profound teaching on the supremacy of love over mere knowledge, and the blessedness of surrender over detached contemplation.

## *—: Key Sanskrit Terms :—*

— ॐ तत सत ॐ —

Let us rest with the Sanskrit as with light filling a room. "**मय्यावेश्य मनो ये मां नित्ययुक्ता उपासते । श्रद्धया परयोपेताः ते मे युक्ततमा मताः ॥** Those who fix their mind on Me with supreme faith, them I regard as most united," says Bhagwāna Shri Krishna. Each word glows with simplicity and warmth.

Now let us lean into the stillness of each Sanskrit word the verse holds, and allow it to become a mirror—not of ideas alone, but of the one who gazes.

— ॐ —

**मय्यावेश्य मनः** (mayyāveśya manaḥ):
- **आवेश्य** (āveśya) carries the sense of immersing, placing, or fixing utterly.
- **मनः** (manaḥ) — the mind, the flow of thought and awareness — is here not merely directed but submerged in the Lord.

Faith of the Highest Kind

Not credulity, but clear fire: *śraddhayā parayopetaḥ.*
श्रद्धया परयोपेताः It is Supreme Shraddha—
श्रद्धा Faith that has been washed in many daily tears,
Tried endlessly by nights without answer.
Faith that knows the idol is a window—the sky a veil.

It's faith that takes holds when senses have begun to be undone;
It is faith which's like a mother-hand in storm.
It grows like Banyan—rooted above as below, fed on Secret-Rain.
It answers doubt not with thunder, but with a widening Dawn.
It is milk drawn from the quiet cow of the heart.
It is the sweetness which sages receive last—and savor till end.

- मय्यावेश्य mayyāveśya portrays a consciousness so steeped in the Divine that it becomes inseparable from Him, like water poured into water.

It is a complete relocation of inner life into the sphere of the sacred.

— ॐ —

नित्ययुक्ताः (nityayuktāḥ):
- नित्यय nitya — eternal, constant;
- युक्ताः yukta — united, yoked.

Those thus described are ever-joined to the Lord, without lapse, without forgetfulness.

Their Yoga is not an occasional act but an uninterrupted state of being, like a river unceasingly flowing to the ocean.

— ॐ —

उपास्ते (upāsate):
- उपास्ना upāsana implies more than prayer or worship in the shallow sense;

it is sustained, reverent dwelling upon the Divine, an active

The Lord-God Bhagwāna

O mortal, reflect on His Face in the Divine-Form Krishna,
Or in the Unseen-Light—in the Formless Braham ॐ
Both are He, Krishna—
—First decide which is the innate way of thy heart—
How really do thou lovest?

Approach by *Murti*, or approach by mirthless sky,
or where both paths meet halfway—
And thou wilt find Krishna standing right there.

O Krishna, Thou meetest us always—
Be we stay whichever way:
Stray this-way, that-way, both-way, full-way or half-way.

He is Both

Thou O Krishna art the smile upon the image idol,
Thou the breeze in the vacant sanctum of the Infinite,
The bell rings for Thee alone—in clay and in cloud alike.

For devotee who loves forms—symbols blossom into sight.
For him who trusts the formless—emptiness itself becomes a full chalice.

presence before the Supreme, a ritual enacted not merely outwardly but inwardly through thought, feeling, and surrender.

— ॐ —

श्रद्धया परया उपेताः (śraddhayā parayā upetāḥ):

- श्रद्धा (śraddhā) — faith — is here crowned with the epithet परया (parayā) — supreme, transcendent.

Such faith is not a wavering hope, but a luminous certainty born from the soul's deeper intuition of the Real.

श्रद्धा is the flame that withstands the winds of doubt and the darkness of reason.

- उपेताः upetāḥ — endowed with, possessed of — suggests that such supreme faith is the very adornment of these devotees.

— ॐ —

ते मे युक्ततमाः मताः (te me yuktatamāḥ matāḥ):

- युक्ततमाः (yuktatamāḥ) — the most perfectly united, the most accomplished in Yoga.

- मम मतः (mama mataḥ) — by me (मम) are considered मत — in my opinion;

i.e., them I deem to be higher.

Thus, the Lord Himself declares that these devotees, who worship God with form, with mind, heart, and unwavering faith, may be counted foremost among Yogis.

*—: In Brief :—*

— ॐ श्रीकृष्णाय नमः ॐ —

Shri Krishna, with a heart full of grace, declares that those devotees who, with their minds ever absorbed in Him and endowed with supreme, unwavering faith, worship Him as the Lord of manifest form, are to be deemed the higher knowers of Yoga.

This is not a mere comparison of outer practices, but a revelation

Oneness

God-with-Form or Formless-God—it matters not;
Remember O mortal: the robe may differ; the wearer is always One.
Either which way, stay yoked (*yukta* युक्त) to Him: Krishna.
युक्ततमा *Yuktatama* is not a mask but the very marrow of a Yogi,
It's a soul that has learnt to see Krishna in everything—
In His Divine-Form and in the Formless ॐ.

of the profound inner movement of the soul. The devotee of this kind, surrenders not only the intellect but the heart, the will, and the entire being at the lotus feet of the Lord.

— ॐ श्रीरामाय नमः ॐ —

Such supreme faith (para-śraddhā) is not blind sentiment; it is the luminous certainty born of inner realization—an unshakable trust in the Lord's reality, His divine play, His all-pervading presence, and His boundless grace.

The devotee thus lives, moves, and breathes in the remembrance of the Lord—His glories, virtues, leelās (divine pastimes), and names—whether amidst the duties of the world or in solitary meditation.

This profound absorption (युक्ततमा yukta-tamah), marked by a seamless union of heart and mind with the Divine, is what marks the supreme Yogi.

— ॐ सुन्दराय नमः ॐ —

The Lord's judgment here is decisive: the path of loving surrender, the path that integrates knowledge, action, and feeling in a stream of pure devotion, is higher—for reasons that will be made clear in the coming verses.

Yet, Shri Krishna, ever compassionate, does not disregard the sincere aspirants who approach Him through the path of the unmanifest Absolute.

With wisdom and tenderness, Bhagwāna will go on in the next verses to elucidate the noble, though more arduous, nature of the jñānī's path, thus guiding Arjuna and all seekers toward a comprehensive understanding of the many ways to reach the Supreme.

— ॐ अदोक्षजाय नमः ॐ —

It is just so that the worship of God-with-form is far easier than worshipping Him in His formless aspect—and consequently is considered a better path.

Remember: In the profound wisdom of Sanātana-Dharma, Jñāna and Bhakti are seen not as rivals but as twin wings of the soul's flight toward the Eternal.

Here, Bhagwāna confirms that the path of loving absorption — mind enraptured, heart steadfast, being surrendered — is a direct and sweet passage to the Infinite.

— ॐ तत सत ॐ —

Before we move on, let us bow in reverence to this sacred verse—a timeless beacon of wisdom guiding seekers for ages. Write it by hand, reflect on its meaning, and chant it aloud, for these sounds alone carry the authenticity of that era. The world may have changed but the living vibration of these Sanskrit sounds still remain as original as they were when Bhagwān Shri Krishna Himself walked the earth and imparted these teachings.

— ॐ —

श्रीभगवानुवाच --
*śrībhagavānuvāca --*

**मय्यावेश्य मनो ये मां नित्ययुक्ता उपासते ।**
**mayyāveśya mano ye māṁ nityayuktā upāsate**
**श्रद्धया परयोपेताः ते मे युक्ततमा मताः ॥१२-२॥**
**śraddhayā parayopetāḥ te me yuktatamā matāḥ (12-2)**

—ॐ—

श्रीभगवानुवाच -- śrībhagavānuvāca --
मय्यावेश्य मनो ये मां नित्ययुक्ता उपासते ।
mayyāveśya mano ye māṁ nityayuktā upāsate
श्रद्धया परयोपेताः ते मे युक्ततमा मताः ॥१२-२॥
śraddhayā parayopetāḥ te me yuktatamā matāḥ (12-2)

ॐ तत्सदिति श्रीमद्भगवद्गीतासूपनिषत्सु ब्रह्मविद्यायां योगशास्त्रे श्रीकृष्णार्जुनसंवादे
om tatsaditi śrīmadbhagavadgītāsūpaniṣatsu brahmavidyāyāṁ yogaśāstre śrīkṛṣṇārjunasaṁvāde
भक्तियोगो नाम द्वादशोऽध्यायः श्लोकः २
bhaktiyogo nāma dvādaśo'dhyāyaḥ ślokaḥ 2

**Om-Tat-Sat—Om (Braham) is the sole Reality. In the Yogic Scripture on the Science-of-Braham, the Shrimada-Bhāgvada-Gītā Upanishad, we hereby conclude Shloka 2 of the Dialogue between Shrī Krishna and Arjuna entitled Bhakti-Yoga, Canto XII.**

— ॐ सत्यवाचे नमः ॐ —

The Hard Long Road to the Formless

Some seek only That which has no name.
Which neither shines nor speaks.
Which gives no sign. No sound. Has no shrine,
No bells, whistle, song.
Ah — how hard this path most sublime.
And many obeisances to thee — if thou art there!

As to the rest—those in flesh—soft and sense-swayed—
They have only known the Seen.
And they only crave the same:
Satt-chitt-ânanda braham in His divine form as Bhagwâna Shri Krishna.

# ॐ गीता श्लोकः १२.३-४ – GĪTĀ VERSE 12.3-4

ॐ श्रीमद्भगवद्गीतासूपनिषत्सु ब्रह्मविद्यायां योगशास्त्रे श्रीकृष्णार्जुनसंवादे
om śrīmadbhagavadgītāsūpaniṣatsu brahmavidyāyāṁ yogaśāstre śrīkṛṣṇārjunasaṁvāde
भक्तियोगो नाम द्वादशोऽध्यायः श्लोकः ३-४
bhaktiyogo nāma dvādaśo'dhyāyaḥ ślokaḥ 3-4

— ॐ —

**ये त्वक्षरमनिर्देश्यमव्यक्तं पर्युपासते ।**
**ye tvakṣaramanirdeśyamavyaktaṁ paryupāsate**
**सर्वत्रगमचिन्त्यञ्च कूटस्थमचलन्ध्रुवम् ॥ १२-३ ॥**
**sarvatragamacintyañca kūṭasthamacalandhruvam** (12-3)

**सन्नियम्येन्द्रियग्रामं सर्वत्र समबुद्धयः ।**
**sanniyamyendriyagrāmaṁ sarvatra samabuddhayaḥ**
**ते प्राप्नुवन्ति मामेव सर्वभूतहिते रताः ॥ १२-४ ॥**
**te prāpnuvanti māmeva sarvabhūtahite ratāḥ** (12-4)

**Those who worship the imperishable, indescribable, unmanifest, omnipresent, eternal, immovable, inconceivable, unalterable form of Mine (Braham)—by controlling well their senses, ever remaining even-minded, devoted to Me as the Ātmā presiding everywhere, and given to all-round welfare of beings everywhere—such too attain only to Me.** (12.3-12.4)

## *—: Word-by-Word :—*

**ये** ye – those who; **तु** tu – but; **अक्षरम्** akṣaram – the imperishable; **अनिर्देश्यं** anirdeśyam – the indefinable; **अव्यक्तम्** avyaktaṁ – the unmanifest; **पर्युपासते** paryupāsate – worship; **सर्वत्र-गम्** sarvatra-gam – all-pervading; **अचिन्त्यम्** acintyam – inconceivable; **च** ca – and; **कूटस्थम्** kūṭastham – unchanging; **अचलम्** acalam – immovable; **ध्रुवम्** dhruvam – eternal.

**सन्नियम्य** sanniyamya – completely controlling; **इन्द्रिय-ग्रामम्** indriya-grāmam – the group of senses; **सर्वत्र** sarvatra – everywhere; **सम-बुद्धयः** sama-buddhayaḥ – those with an equal mind; **ते** te – they; **प्राप्नुवन्ति** prāpnuvanti – attain; **माम् एव** mām eva – me alone; **सर्व-भूत-हिते** sarva-bhūta-hite – in the welfare of all beings; **रताः** ratāḥ – engaged.

## *—: Understanding The Verse :—*

— ॐ श्रीकृष्णाय नमः ॐ —

In these luminous verses, Bhagwāna Shri Krishna turns His compassionate gaze upon those who tread the austere path of adoration toward the Nirguna Braham—the attributeless, formless Absolute.

Here, the Lord describes the noble qualities and disciplines of such seekers: the restraint of the senses, the steadfast cultivation of even-mindedness, and the unwavering commitment to the welfare of all beings.

These devotees contemplate the imperishable, all-pervading, changeless Braham, seeking union through self-identification with that which transcends all names, forms, and limitations.

While the path of bhakti—directed toward the manifest form of the Divine—is marked by love and surrender, this path is one of profound intellectual discernment, inner detachment, and subtle realization.

Most humans being what they are, this path is not in the mental capacity of all.

— ॐ श्रीरामाय नमः ॐ —

Shri Krishna's words affirm that those who persevere on this challenging path do very much reach Him—for the Supreme and the Absolute are not two but one, known and attained according to the fitness and disposition of the aspirant.

Let us never un-remember that satt-chitt-ānanda braham is the formless ocean of consciousness—and His manifest human form is that of Bhagwāna Shri Krishna and Bhagwāna Shri Rāma. Braham assumed these manifest forms for the facilitation of us humans—who find impossible to meditate upon the formless and need a divine form at where to direct our love and devotion.

This verse sets the stage for a deeper exploration of the comparative ease and beauty of the path of loving devotion, which Krishna will soon unfold.

## *—: Key Sanskrit Terms :—*

— ॐ तत सत ॐ —

Let us hear the Sanskrit as with the unseen-wind sweeping through seen branches—and thusly known. ““ये त्वक्षरमनिर्देश्यमव्यक्तं पर्युपासते । सर्वत्रगमचिन्त्यञ्च कूटस्थमचलन्ध्रुवम् ॥...Those who worship the imperishable, unmanifest, self-controlled, equal-minded—they too reach Me...” Each syllable carries austerity, distance, subtle devotion.

Now let us bend close to the verse, like a listener to a conch's song, and hearken to the resonances held within its Sanskrit voice—each word a portal to unseen realms.

— ॐ —

अक्षरम् अनिर्देश्यम् (akṣaram anirdeśyam) :

- अक्षरम् (akṣaram) points to the Imperishable — that which undergoes no decay, no diminution. It is beyond all transience, the very substratum of existence itself.

- अनिर्देश्यम् (anirdeśyam) — that which cannot be indicated or pointed out — highlights the formlessness and inaccessibility of this Reality to the mind that seeks to name and classify.

Here, the अक्षर akṣara is not simply beyond destruction, but also beyond conceptual grasp.

— ॐ —

अव्यक्तम् पर्युपासते (avyaktaṁ paryupāsate):

- अव्यक्तम् (avyaktam) — the Unmanifest — is that which neither mind can conceive nor senses perceive.

- परोपासन (paryupāsana), as earlier noted, is the deeply reverent, sustained worship.

To worship the अव्यक्तम् avyaktam is to adore that which has no form, to love without an object of vision — a supreme act of transcendental faith and inner stillness.

— ॐ —

सर्वत्रगम् अचिन्त्यम् (sarvatragam acintyam):

- सर्वत्रगम् (sarvatragam) — that which goes everywhere, is omnipresent, pervading all without division.

- अचिन्त्यम् (acintyam) — inconceivable — emphasizes that this Reality cannot be thought out by the intellect.

The true essence is reached not by discursive reasoning, but through direct spiritual intuition (अपरोक्ष अनुभूति aparokṣa anubhūti).

— ॐ —

कूटस्थम् अचलम् ध्रुवम् (kūṭastham acalam dhruvam):

- कूटस्थम् (kūṭastham) — the Immutable — like the anvil upon which changes occur but which itself remains unaffected;

- अचलम् (acalam) — unmoving,

- ध्रुवम् (dhruvam) — eternal and firm — further portray the absolute stillness and permanence of Braham amidst the whirl of माया Māyā's flux.

— ॐ —

सन्नियम्येन्द्रियग्रामम् (sanniyamyendriyagrāmam):

- इन्द्रियग्राम (indriyagrāma) — the ग्राम 'village' or 'collection' of इन्द्रिय senses-organs — must be completely governed (सन्नियम्य sanniyamya).

The senses, by nature outward-turning, must be reined inward, for the subtle Reality is not captured by external pursuit.

— ॐ —

सर्वत्र समबुद्धयः (sarvatra samabuddhayaḥ):
Those whose
-बुद्धि (buddhi) — intellect or understanding — remains
- सम (sama) — even, equal — everywhere and toward all beings.
Such even-mindedness (समता samatā) is the signature of one who sees the One Self shining in all forms.

— ॐ —

सर्वभूतहिते रताः (sarvabhūtahite ratāḥ):
Meaning finding joy (रताः, ratāḥ) in the welfare (हित, hita) of all beings (सर्वभूत, sarvabhūta).
Their devotion manifests not in isolation but in active, universal compassion — seeing all beings as extensions of the same Self.
Lest you forget, भूत bhūt beings, are all beings—not just humans.

*—: In Brief :—*

— ॐ श्रीकृष्णाय नमः ॐ —

Bhagwāna Shri Krishna, with infinite tenderness, acknowledges the noble souls who, through disciplined effort and profound reflection, worship the imperishable, undefinable, and unmanifest Braham.

Such aspirants, having subdued the restless senses, abide in unwavering equanimity, unshaken by the opposites of life. Their hearts, expanded in universal compassion, rejoice in the welfare of all, seeing in every creature the one indivisible Self.

— ॐ श्रीरामाय नमः ॐ —

To them, the Absolute is not an abstraction, but their very essence—the immortal Self that pervades the entire cosmos like the subtle ether, untouched by change or decay.

The terms employed here:
- सर्वत्रग sarvatraga (all-pervading),
- अनिर्देश्यं anirdeśya (indescribable),
- कूटस्थम् kūṭastha (changeless),
- ध्रुव dhruva (eternal),
- अचल acala (immovable),
- अव्यक्त avyakta (unmanifest), and

- अक्षर akṣara (imperishable)—paint a portrait of the transcendent Reality beyond all sensory and conceptual grasp.

The seeker on this path, through sustained contemplation, dissolves the illusion of separateness, seeing no "other," no division between self and world.

Such realization blossoms into spontaneous goodwill toward all, for when one perceives the same Self everywhere, how can there be any boundary between one's own welfare and that of others?

— ॐ पुण्यश्रवणकीर्तनाय नमः ॐ —

Yet, Shri Krishna, ever the compassionate teacher, gently foreshadows the inherent difficulty of this way.

While both the path of nirguna-bhakti and that of saguna-bhakti lead to Him, the former is arduous, suited only to those who can transcend the bodily sense of self and abide unwaveringly in the subtle, formless Absolute.

The Lord will soon reveal that the path of loving devotion to the manifest form—where the heart can cling to the Divine in form, name, and leelā—is more accessible to embodied beings and crowned with the sweetness of divine intimacy.

— ॐ महाधनुष्मते नमः ॐ —

These verses honor the grandeur of both paths, while quietly preparing the aspirant to hear of the supreme excellence and tenderness of the path of saguna-bhakti.

In the unfolding verses, Shri Krishna will illumine the soul's natural inclination toward love, and the ease with which loving devotion carries one across the ocean of Sansara.

— ॐ तत सत ॐ —

Before moving on, let us once more bow in deep reverence before these sacred verses of the Bhagavad-Gītā, an eternal beacon of wisdom that ceaselessly illumines the path of seekers. Engage with its form—inscribe it with your own hand, let your heart dwell upon its meaning, and raise your voice in its chanting—for within these syllables echoes the undying proclamation delivered millennia ago on the battlefield of Kurukshetra. These words, transmitted unchanged across the unbroken chain of generations, form a living bridge, linking us to that sanctified era when Bhagwāna Shri Krishna Himself walked this earth and bestowed this divine teaching. Through the luminous vibration of these sacred Sanskrit sounds, we are drawn nearer to His timeless presence, touching the very heartbeat of the Eternal.

— ॐ —

ये त्वक्षरमनिर्देश्यमव्यक्तं पर्युपासते ।
ye tvakṣaramanirdeśyamavyaktaṁ paryupāsate
सर्वत्रगमचिन्त्यञ्च कूटस्थमचलन्ध्रुवम् ॥ १२-३॥
sarvatragamacintyañca kūṭasthamacalandhruvam (12-3)

**सन्नियम्येन्द्रियग्रामं सर्वत्र समबुद्धयः ।**
**sanniyamyendriyagrāmaṁ sarvatra samabuddhayaḥ**
**ते प्राप्नुवन्ति मामेव सर्वभूतहिते रताः ॥१२-४॥**
**te prāpnuvanti māmeva sarvabhūtahite ratāḥ (12-4)**

— ॐ —

ये त्वक्षरमनिर्देश्यमव्यक्तं पर्युपासते ।
ye tvakṣaramanirdeśyamavyaktaṁ paryupāsate
सर्वत्रगमचिन्त्यञ्च कूटस्थमचलन्ध्रुवम् ॥१२-३॥
sarvatragamacintyañca kūṭasthamacalandhruvam (12-3)
सन्नियम्येन्द्रियग्रामं सर्वत्र समबुद्धयः ।
sanniyamyendriyagrāmaṁ sarvatra samabuddhayaḥ
ते प्राप्नुवन्ति मामेव सर्वभूतहिते रताः ॥१२-४॥
te prāpnuvanti māmeva sarvabhūtahite ratāḥ (12-4)

ॐ तत्सदिति श्रीमद्भगवद्गीतासूपनिषत्सु ब्रह्मविद्यायां योगशास्त्रे श्रीकृष्णार्जुनसंवादे
om tatsaditi śrīmadbhagavadgītāsūpaniṣatsu brahmavidyāyāṁ yogaśāstre śrīkṛṣṇārjunasaṁvāde
भक्तियोगो नाम द्वादशोऽध्यायः श्लोकः ३-४
bhaktiyogo nāma dvādaśo'dhyāyaḥ ślokaḥ 3-4

**Om-Tat-Sat—Om (Braham) is the sole Reality. In the Yogic Scripture on the Science-of-Braham, the Shrimada-Bhāgvada-Gītā Upanishad, we hereby conclude Shloka 3-4 of the Dialogue between Shrī Krishna and Arjuna entitled Bhakti-Yoga, Canto XII.**

— ॐ सत्यवाचाय नमः ॐ —

## The Lord's Invisible Measure

"Those who paryupasate पर्युपासते the Imperishable"—says the voice of Krishna,
"The akṣaram anirdeśyam avyaktam अक्षरम्-निर्देश्यं-अव्यक्तम्,
The sarvatragam-acintyam सर्वत्र-गम्-अचिन्त्यम्
—Everywhere pervaded and beyond the purview of mind's ponderings,
kutaastham-acalam-dhruvam कूटस्थम्-अचलम्-ध्रुवम् —
The anvilled, unmoving, sure— prapnuvanti-mam-eva प्राप्नुवन्ति-माम्-एव
Those Devotees too attain only to Me." —
Thus the Sky lays down its rule with no edge, no decree.
Thus the wind explains its grammar by blowing through the reeds.
Thus Love learns to bow before what no hand can hold.

Instruction: Rein the Senses

"Saddle thy horses," saith the quiet Master.
Samniyamya-indriya-gramam सन्नियम्य-इन्द्रिय-ग्रामम्—gather the village of the senses;
Bid them sit at dusk, salt and bread, no quarrel, no raid.
Let taste be a servant, not a king,
Let sight be a window, not a thief.
Make breath the constable of wandering thought,
and thy heart the stern magistrate.
Then shall desire grow tame—and the Self luminous.

Commandment: the Even Vision

सर्वत्र-सम-बुद्धयः Sarvatra samabuddhayaḥ—
Stay as the One-mind across all weathers.
Praise does not swell it; nor does the blame bruise.
Gold is earth with a rumor. Earth is gold without a rumor.
Friend and stranger stand in one light.
Pleasure and pain share the same threshold.

It is not Coldness, but a clear warmth spread evenly.
Thusly is the scale balanced by the invisible hand.
Thus is the mirror of the Self wiped—and left to shine as itself.

Promise: The Quiet Attainment

O, it is so formidable—this way.
Now, what be the wage?
No wages—only the fall of distance to Me.

ते-प्राप्नुवन्ति-माम्-एव Te-prapnuvanti-mam-eva—For such alone ever reach Me.
not as a region won, but the mislaid recalled back Home.

The house was never sold; the key was always in the lock.
The tenant and the owner now shake hands—and vanish into the One.
In the emptied room, not two, but only a single-flame remains.
Its name is Thou.

Tat-tvam-asi तत् त्वम् असि, O mortal, Tat-tvam-asi.
That Thou Art.

— ॐ तत सत ॐ —

## ॐ गीता श्लोकः १२.५ – GĪTĀ VERSE 12.5

ॐ श्रीमद्भगवद्गीतासूपनिषत्सु ब्रह्मविद्यायां योगशास्त्रे श्रीकृष्णार्जुनसंवादे
om śrīmadbhagavadgītāsūpaniṣatsu brahmavidyāyāṁ yogaśāstre śrīkṛṣṇārjunasaṁvāde
भक्तियोगो नाम द्वादशोऽध्यायः श्लोकः ५
bhaktiyogo nāma dvādaśo'dhyāyaḥ ślokaḥ 5

— ॐ —

**क्लेशोऽधिकतरस्तेषामव्यक्तासक्तचेतसाम् ।**
**kleśo'dhikatarasteṣāmavyaktāsaktacetasām**
**अव्यक्ता हि गतिर्दुःखं देहवद्भिरवाप्यते ॥१२-५॥**
**avyaktā hi gatirduḥkhaṁ dehavadbhiravāpyate** (12-5)

**However the effort is much harder for those who perform their worship attached to Brahama. The devotion to the Unmanifest is attained only with great difficulty by a soul—having become manifest in bodily form.** (12.5)

*—: Word-by-Word :—*

क्लेशः kleśaḥ – hardship; अधिकतरः adhikataraḥ – greater; तेषाम् teṣām – for those; अव्यक्त-आसक्त-चेतसाम् avyakta-āsakta-cetasām – whose minds are attached to the unmanifest; अव्यक्ता avyaktaḥ – the unmanifest; हि hi – indeed; गतिः gatiḥ – path; दुःखम् duḥkham – is difficult; देहवत्-भिः dehavadbhiḥ – for those with a physical body; अवाप्यते avāpyate – to attain.

***—: Understanding The Verse :—***

— ॐ श्रीकृष्णाय नमः ॐ —

In this verse, Bhagwāna Shri Krishna reveals an important truth about the inherent challenge of approaching the Unmanifest, attributeless Braham. Having acknowledged in the preceding verses that those who worship the Nirguna Braham do indeed reach Him, Krishna now explains the arduous nature of that path.

The difficulty arises from the embodied condition of the aspirant—so long as the soul remains identified with the body, the senses, and the mutable world, the transcendence required for realization of the formless Absolute proves exceptionally demanding.

This verse highlights the contrast between the two modes of worship: while meditation upon the unmanifest Absolute requires profound renunciation and inner purity, by contrast the bhakti directed toward the same Absolute—but in His manifest presence on earth as Bhagwāna Shri Krishna, the personal form of the same ocean of consciousness called satt-chitt-ānanda braham—allows for a speedier, more accessible, grace-filled path to the same goal!

Thus, Krishna prepares the ground for teaching the relative ease and beauty of saguna-bhakti in the verses that follow.

*—: Key Sanskrit Terms :—*

Let us linger with the Sanskrit as with stones upon a steep path. "क्लेशोऽधिकतरस्तेषामव्यक्तासक्तचेतसाम् । अव्यक्ता हि गतिर्दुःखं देहवद्भिरवाप्यते ॥ Hard is the way of the unmanifest; embodied beings find it to be difficult." Each word admits the onerous weight of unseen abstractions.

The verse does not arrive like a chisel meeting stone. It gathers around us like the misty twilight. The Sanskrit is the hush within it, each word a soft turning of dusk into night. Let us illuminate the verse through its core Sanskrit expressions, revealing their layered meaning:

— ॐ —

क्लेशः अधिकतरः (kleśaḥ adhikataraḥ):
- क्लेशः (kleśaḥ) denotes affliction, toil, suffering — not simply external hardship but an inner weariness born of subtle struggling.
- अधिकतरः (adhikataraḥ) means 'greater' or 'more intense.'

Together, this phrase highlights that the burden borne by the aspirants toward the Unmanifest is particularly heavy, the path strewn with unseen trials.

— ॐ —

अव्यक्तासक्तचेतसाम् (avyaktāsaktacetasām):

Those whose चेतस (cetas) — consciousness — is आसक्त (āsakta) — attached, absorbed — in the अव्यक्त (avyakta) — the Unmanifest.

The description is gentle but profound: even though the mind clings to the formless Truth, its very formlessness becomes a challenge for the embodied seeker.

— ॐ —

अव्यक्ता हि गतिः दुःखम् (avyaktā hi gatiḥ duḥkham):

The path गतिः (gatiḥ) to the Unmanifest is rife with दुःखम् (duḥkham) — painful, difficult.
- हि (Hi) underscores it as a natural law — not a flaw of the path, but an inevitability arising from the nature of embodiment.

— ॐ —

देहवद्भिः अवाप्यते (dehavadbhiḥ avāpyate):

For those who are देहवत् (dehavat) — possessing a body — realization अवाप्यते of the Unmanifest is attained only with difficulty.

The word देहवत् implies that embodiment itself—with its gross senses, restless mind, and tendencies born of material nature (प्रकृति prakṛti)—innately imposes a thick veil between the soul and the pure Reality.

*—: In Brief :—*

— ॐ श्रीकृष्णाय नमः ॐ —

Bhagwāna Shri Krishna, ever the compassionate guide, candidly acknowledges that the path of those who fix their minds upon the unmanifest, imperishable Braham is indeed a steep and rugged ascent.

The pronoun तेषाम् teṣām, qualified by अव्यक्त-आसक्त-चेतसाम् avyakta-sakta-cetasām—those whose minds are attached to the Unmanifest—points unmistakably to the aspirants of the previous verses who seek union with the attributeless Absolute.

— ॐ महाभुजाय नमः ॐ —

The Lord makes it clear that as long as one remains centered in the body, entangled in the identifications and limitations of the embodied state, the comprehension and realization of the Absolute is exceedingly difficult.

The formless Braham, being beyond name, form, quality, and relationality, eludes the grasp of the senses and even the conceptual intellect.

To abide in that realization demands a mind unsullied by the waves of passion (rajas) and inertia (tamas), and a heart free from the subtlest trace of egoism or attachment.

Such purity is rare, and its attainment very hard-won. Thus, the struggle of the aspirant on this path is not just a matter of intellectual effort but a profound purification of the entire being—a stripping away of all that conceals the ever-present Reality.

— ॐ भगवते नमः ॐ —

Mind it, Shri Krishna's intention here is not to disparage the path of the jñāni, but to highlight the merciful accessibility of the path of bhakti.

For the devotee who surrenders to the Lord with form and attributes, the Lord Himself becomes the helper, lifting the devotee over the turbulent sea of becoming.

As the Gītā will soon reveal, the path of loving devotion, sustained by divine grace, removes the burden from the aspirant's shoulders and replaces it with a sweetness that melts all resistance.

— ॐ धन्वन्तरये नमः ॐ —

Thus, Krishna gently leads Arjuna—and all of us—toward the understanding that while the unmanifest path is indeed noble, the path of surrender to the personal Lord, walked with love and faith, offers a supreme ease and swiftness of attainment.

In the following verses, the Lord will unfold the contours of this blessed path, calling the hearts of seekers to repose in the arms of divine love.

— ॐ तत सत ॐ —

Before we move on, let us bow in reverence to this sacred verse—a timeless beacon of wisdom guiding seekers for ages. Write it by hand, reflect on its meaning, and chant it aloud, for these sounds alone carry the authenticity of that era. The world may have changed but the living vibration of these Sanskrit sounds still remain as original as they were when Bhagwān Shri Krishna Himself walked the earth and imparted these teachings.

— ॐ —

**क्लेशोऽधिकतरस्तेषामव्यक्तासक्तचेतसाम् ।**
**kleśo'dhikatarasteṣāmavyaktāsaktacetasām**
**अव्यक्ता हि गतिर्दुःखं देहवद्भिरवाप्यते ॥१२-५॥**
**avyaktā hi gatirduḥkhaṁ dehavadbhiravāpyate (12-5)**

— ॐ —

क्लेशोऽधिकतरस्तेषामव्यक्तासक्तचेतसाम् ।
kleśo'dhikatarasteṣāmavyaktāsaktacetasām
अव्यक्ता हि गतिर्दुःखं देहवद्भिरवाप्यते ॥१२-५॥
avyaktā hi gatirduḥkhaṁ dehavadbhiravāpyate (12-5)

ॐ तत्सदिति श्रीमद्भगवद्गीतासूपनिषत्सु ब्रह्मविद्यायां योगशास्त्रे श्रीकृष्णार्जुनसंवादे
om tatsaditi śrīmadbhagavadgītāsūpaniṣatsu brahmavidyāyāṁ yogaśāstre śrīkṛṣṇārjunasaṁvāde
भक्तियोगो नाम द्वादशोऽध्यायः श्लोकः ५
bhaktiyogo nāma dvādaśo'dhyāyaḥ ślokaḥ 5

**Om-Tat-Sat—Om (Braham) is the sole Reality. In the Yogic Scripture on the Science-of-Braham, the Shrimada-Bhāgvada-Gītā Upanishad, we hereby conclude Shloka 5 of the Dialogue between Shrī Krishna and Arjuna entitled Bhakti-Yoga, Canto XII.**

## ॐ गीता श्लोकः १२.६-७ – Gītā Verse 12.6-7

ॐ श्रीमद्भगवद्गीतासूपनिषत्सु ब्रह्मविद्यायां योगशास्त्रे श्रीकृष्णार्जुनसंवादे
om śrīmadbhagavadgītāsūpaniṣatsu brahmavidyāyāṁ yogaśāstre śrīkṛṣṇārjunasaṁvāde
भक्तियोगो नाम द्वादशोऽध्यायः श्लोकः ६-७
bhaktiyogo nāma dvādaśo'dhyāyaḥ ślokaḥ 6-7

— ॐ —

**ये तु सर्वाणि कर्माणि मयि संन्यस्य मत्पराः ।**
**ye tu sarvāṇi karmāṇi mayi saṁnyasya matparāḥ**
**अनन्येनैव योगेन मां ध्यायन्त उपासते ॥ १२-६॥**
**ananyenaiva yogena māṁ dhyāyanta upāsate** (12-6)

**तेषामहं समुद्धर्ता मृत्युसंसारसागरात् ।**
**teṣāmahaṁ samuddhartā mṛtyusaṁsārasāgarāt**
**भवामि नचिरात्पार्थ मय्यावेशितचेतसाम् ॥ १२-७॥**
**bhavāmi nacirātpārtha mayyāveśitacetasām** (12-7)

**By contrast those who are attached to my manifest form; who, surrendering all action in Me, worship Me with unflinching devotion; who, through meditation, have fixed their minds intently upon Me—them I quickly redeem from this ocean of transmigratory existence which is fraught with miseries of births and deaths.** (12.6-12.7)

*—: Word-by-Word :—*

ये ye – those who; तु tu – but; सर्वाणि sarvāṇi – all; कर्माणि karmāṇi – actions; मयि mayi – in me; संन्यस्य saṁnyasya – renouncing; मत्पराः matparāḥ – dedicated to me; अनन्येन ananyena – with undivided; एव eva – indeed; योगेन yogena – through yoga; माम् mām – on me; ध्यायन्तः dhyāyantaḥ – meditating; उपासते upāsate – worship.

तेषाम् teṣām – for them; अहम् aham – I; समुद्धर्ता samuddhartā – the deliverer; मृत्युः-संसार-सागरात् mṛtyu-saṁsāra-sāgarāt – from the ocean of mortal existence; भवामि bhavāmi – I become; नचिरात् na cirāt – without delay; पार्थ pārtha – O son of Pritha (Arjuna); मयि mayi – in me; आवेशित-चेतसाम् āveśita-cetasām – whose minds are absorbed.

*—: Understanding The Verse :—*

— ॐ श्रीकृष्णाय नमः ॐ —

In these luminous verses, Bhagwāna Shri Krishna turns to extol the blessedness of those devotees who surrender themselves wholly unto Him—the Lord with attributes and form.

Unlike the arduous path of contemplation upon the unmanifest Absolute, the path of saguna-bhakti is marked by deep reliance upon divine grace.

Here, the Lord promises that those who, with single-minded love, surrender all their actions unto Him, worship Him with unwavering devotion, and keep their minds steadfastly fixed upon Him, will be swiftly delivered from the ocean of saṁsāra—the endless cycle of birth and death.

— ॐ श्रीरामाय नमः ॐ —

Krishna thus reveals the tender-hearted and protective nature of the Divine, assuring that He Himself becomes the savior and refuge of those who approach Him in loving surrender.

These verses elevate bhakti not merely as a practice, but as a profound covenant between the soul and the Supreme, where the Lord, moved by the selfless love of the devotee, takes upon Himself the responsibility for the devotee's liberation.

Shri Krishna assures: "For those who worship Me with unflinching devotion, I am both the path and the goal; I carry them swiftly across the ocean of suffering and welcome them into the blissful infinity of My Being."

<u>*—: Key Sanskrit Terms :—*</u>

Let us rest with the Sanskrit as with a hand clasped firmly in ours. "ये तु सर्वाणि कर्माणि मयि संन्यस्य मत्पराः । अनन्येनैव योगेन मां ध्यायन्त उपासते ॥... Those who dedicate all acts to Me, who worship with single-minded yoga—I quickly lift them from ocean of death and rebirth..." Each syllable reassures with saving nearness.

Some verses shout their truth; these ones whisper; their Sanskrit whispers like a tide pulling at our ankles—firm, quiet, and impossible to ignore. Now then let us continue our sacred journey and look at the Sanskrit terms:

— ॐ —

ये तु सर्वाणि कर्माणि मयि संन्यस्य (ye tu sarvāṇi karmāṇi mayi saṁnyasya) — "But those who, having offered all their actions entirely unto Me..."

- तु ये — But they who, a contrast to those with lesser or distracted devotion.

- सर्वाणि कर्माणि (sarvāṇi karmāṇi) — all actions, every work, duty, responsibility, movement of life — physical, mental, emotional.

- संन्यस्य (saṁnyasya) — having surrendered, renounced, laid down, handed over.
- मयि (mayi) — unto Me, the Divine, the Supreme Self, the Eternal Witness.

This is the spirit of total surrender — not the abandonment of action, but the offering of all action. Nothing is withheld. Every act becomes sacred when it is emptied of ego and filled with the intent to serve the Divine. There is no separation between secular and sacred; life itself becomes yajña — a continuous offering.

— ॐ —

मत्पराः (matparāḥ) — "Whose whole being is centered upon Me as the highest aim..."

- मत्पराः (mat-parāḥ) — Those who make Me their Supreme Purpose, for whom I am the final refuge, the ultimate goal, the all-in-all.

This is exclusive devotion. Not diluted by worldly ambitions, not shared with lesser loyalties. The devotee's inner compass always points to the Divine.

All roads lead to Him, all desires are transfigured into the single flame of God-love. The Divine is not one among many — He is the One without a second.

— ॐ —

अनन्येनैव योगेन (ananyenaiva yogena) — "And who, with unwavering Yoga, are ever united with Me alone..."

- अनन्येन (ananyena) — without another, without secondness, without distraction.
- एव (eva) — indeed, surely, emphasizing exclusivity.
- योगेन (yogena) — by Yoga, the inner discipline and union with the Divine.

This is अनन्य-योग (ananya-yoga) — the Yoga of undivided love and undistracted focus.

The heart does not run after alternatives. No backup gods, no fallback plans. The mind is yoked to Krishna alone, as a river flows to the ocean without branching.

It is not simply concentration — it is consecration.

— ॐ —

मां ध्यायन्तः उपासते (māṁ dhyāyantaḥ upāsate) — "Meditating upon Me and worshipping Me with steadfast devotion..."

- मां (mām) — Me, the Supreme Divine Person.
- ध्यायन्तः (dhyāyantaḥ) — meditating, holding Me in constant inner vision.

-उपासते (upāsate) — worshipping, serving Me with love and reverence.

This is not mechanical repetition. Dhyāna is the soul's gaze upon the Eternal; upāsanā is the soul's embrace of the Beloved.

The Lord is not a distant deity but an indwelling presence. Such devotees live in Him — think, breathe, move in the current of His presence. Their worship is both inward flame and outer action.

— ॐ —

तेषामहं समुद्धर्ता मृत्युसंसारसागरात् (teṣām ahaṁ samuddhartā mṛtyu-saṁsāra-sāgarāt) — "For them, I am the Deliverer — lifting them out of the ocean of birth and death..."

- तेषाम् (teṣām) — For those, such devoted souls.

- अहम् (aham) — I, the Divine Himself.

- समुद्धर्ता (samuddhartā) — the Uplifter, the Rescuer, the One who draws them out.

- मृत्युसंसारसागरात् (mṛtyu-saṁsāra-sāgarāt) — from the ocean of saṁsāra and death — from the deep, dark waters of rebirth, pain, and forgetfulness.

The Lord does not leave the devotee to struggle alone.

He does not merely send a boat — He becomes the boat.

He plunges into the waters to lift the soul to the shore of liberation.

This is the Lord's vow: to deliver those who have surrendered fully, who depend on Him with every heartbeat.

— ॐ —

मय्यावेशितचेतसाम् (mayyāveśita-cetasām) —

"Whose minds and hearts are wholly absorbed in Me..."

- मयि (mayi) — in Me, the Divine.

- आवेशित (āveśita) — immersed, absorbed, completely filled.

- चेतसाम् (cetasām) — of those whose consciousness, mind-heart-awareness.

Their citta is not wandering in the forest of desires. It is a still lake reflecting only the image of the Divine.

Their inner world is no longer a battleground of conflicting tendencies — it is a sanctum where only God dwells.

In such absorption, liberation is not merely a future promise — it is already present, here and now.



*—: In Brief :—*

Bhagwāna Shri Krishna draws here a radiant contrast by declaring that those who, renouncing all sense of agency, surrender every action unto Him, and worship Him with unwavering devotion, are speedily carried across the turbulent ocean of saṁsāra by His own compassionate hand.

The particle तु tu ("however") at the start of verse 12.6 serves to set apart these blessed devotees from those who struggle along the path of the Unmanifest.

While the jñāni strives through austere effort to grasp the inconceivable Absolute, the bhakta casts himself wholly upon the mercy of the Lord, recognizing Krishna as the supreme refuge, the dearest friend, and the all-encompassing goal.

— ॐ श्रीरामाय नमः ॐ —

The phrase मत्पराः mat-parāḥ ("depending exclusively on Me") reveals a heart surrendered in total trust—one that, like Prahlāda of old, remains unmoved even in the face of trials, perceiving every joy and sorrow as a gift from the Beloved.

The true bhakta sees himself not as the doer but as an instrument निमित्त (nimitta) in the hands of the Divine, performing all duties in accordance with dharma, without pride, and without claim to the fruits of action.

This is the meaning of surrendering all actions to the Lord—not a withdrawal from life, but a transfiguration of life, where every thought, word, and deed is offered at His feet.

— ॐ जामदग्न्य महादर्पदलनाय नमः ॐ —

अनन्येन एव योगेन ananyena eva yogena ("with single-minded devotion, the yoga of absorption") describes that rare love in which the devotee's heart knows no other; it is a love unstained by selfishness or the fickleness of desire, a love so complete that the remembrance of the Lord becomes as constant and natural as one's own breathing.

Such devotion expresses itself not merely in silent contemplation, but in the joyous acts of bhakti: singing the Lord's glories, chanting His holy names, recounting His leelās, and thus keeping the heart ever attuned to His presence.

— ॐ खरध्वंसिने नमः ॐ —

In these verses, Shri Krishna not only praises the devotee's surrender but assures His own active role as the redeemer.

The Lord does not stand aloof, demanding the aspirant's solitary effort; rather, He rushes to the aid of His lover, lifting him from the depths of saṁsāra.

It is this divine assurance that marks bhakti as supremely accessible, infusing it with a sweetness and intimacy unmatched by the path of the formless Absolute.

Krishna prepares Arjuna—and through him, all us seekers—to recognize the unparalleled grace and power of loving devotion. In the verses to come, He will tenderly instruct on the various ways this devotion can be cultivated, opening the gates of liberation to all who turn toward Him with a sincere heart.

— ॐ तत सत ॐ —

Before we move on, let us bow in reverence to this sacred verse. Write it by hand, reflect on its meaning, chant it aloud, make it your own.

— ॐ —

**ये तु सर्वाणि कर्माणि मयि संन्यस्य मत्पराः ।**
ye tu sarvāṇi karmāṇi mayi saṁnyasya matparāḥ
**अनन्येनैव योगेन मां ध्यायन्त उपासते ॥ १२-६ ॥**
ananyenaiva yogena māṁ dhyāyanta upāsate (12-6)
**तेषामहं समुद्धर्ता मृत्युसंसारसागरात् ।**
teṣāmahaṁ samuddhartā mṛtyusaṁsārasāgarāt
**भवामि नचिरात्पार्थ मय्यावेशितचेतसाम् ॥ १२-७ ॥**
bhavāmi nacirātpārtha mayyāveśitacetasām (12-7)

— ॐ —

ये तु सर्वाणि कर्माणि मयि संन्यस्य मत्पराः ।
ye tu sarvāṇi karmāṇi mayi saṁnyasya matparāḥ
अनन्येनैव योगेन मां ध्यायन्त उपासते ॥ १२-६ ॥
ananyenaiva yogena māṁ dhyāyanta upāsate (12-6)
तेषामहं समुद्धर्ता मृत्युसंसारसागरात् ।
teṣāmahaṁ samuddhartā mṛtyusaṁsārasāgarāt
भवामि नचिरात्पार्थ मय्यावेशितचेतसाम् ॥ १२-७ ॥
bhavāmi nacirātpārtha mayyāveśitacetasām (12-7)

ॐ तत्सदिति श्रीमद्भगवद्गीतासूपनिषत्सु ब्रह्मविद्यायां योगशास्त्रे श्रीकृष्णार्जुनसंवादे
om tatsaditi śrīmadbhagavadgītāsūpaniṣatsu brahmavidyāyāṁ yogaśāstre śrīkṛṣṇārjunasaṁvāde
भक्तियोगो नाम द्वादशोऽध्यायः श्लोकः ६-७
bhaktiyogo nāma dvādaśo'dhyāyaḥ ślokaḥ 6-7

**Om-Tat-Sat—Om (Braham) is the sole Reality. In the Yogic Scripture on the Science-of-Braham, the Shrimada-Bhāgvada-Gītā Upanishad, we hereby conclude Shloka 6-7 of the Dialogue between Shrī Krishna and Arjuna entitled Bhakti-Yoga, Canto XII.**

— ॐ माधवाय नमः ॐ —

Samsara-Sagara संसार सागर —The Ocean Most Formidable

This life—is not a garden.
It's a Ocean vicious dark, in a perennial churn.
Zested with birth, salted with tears of death,
Spiced in between with joys-&-aches.
O, how to ford this terrible sea?
The wise do not just keep splashing around in it—
Unto Krishna, they first make their cession.

Shri Krishna's Sure Promise:

"Those who—सर्वाणि कर्माणि मयि संन्यस्य *sarvani-karmani-mayi-samnyasya*—
lay all deeds in My palm;
those who—मत्पराः *mat-parah*—keep Me as their only North—
those who—अनन्येनैव योगेन *ananyena-yogena*—dwell unbroken in Me,
मां ध्यायन्त उपासते *mam-dhyayanta-upasate*—worship through thought's steady flame
—तेषामहं समुद्धर्ता मृत्युसंसारसागरात *tesham-aham-samuddharta-mrtyu-samsara-sagarata*—
Them I lift from this manifest ocean of sorrows—नचिरात *na-chirat*—
swiftly, O Partha."

Surrender the Whole Loom to Him

Aye, surrender completely, with not even one thread held back—
not the bright threads of joy, not the dark skeins of pain.
—कर्माणि संन्यस्य *Karmani-samnyasya*—surrender all karmas,
let the whole loom be the Lord's—weave no pattern for thyself,

Every breath, every errand, every bread-breaking, every night-watch—
if placed in Him, becomes untarnished shining golden.
Thusly doth the Common become Holy,
and then the holy within thee, O mortal,
becomes as common as thy every breath.

Point To the North—and Then Do Not Stray

Stay minded towards Me alone: the One-North --मत्पराः *Mat-parah*
Nay, not just a casual ramble. Not simply a passing swing,
Nor just some seasonal vow. Or simply that plain old mood, —
But be a fixed star—a pole unmoved through the drifting clouds.

Let winds of opinion blow—the mast does not turn.
Let tempests of fortune roar—the compass will not ever waver.
Such constancy is not stiffness but ripened love—
the fruit that has learned the sweetness of the One-True-Sun: Krishna.
This is the mind that can walk the whole world over—
But without ever losing its road.

## ॐ गीता श्लोकः १२.८ – GĪTĀ VERSE 12.8

ॐ श्रीमद्भगवद्गीतासूपनिषत्सु ब्रह्मविद्यायां योगशास्त्रे श्रीकृष्णार्जुनसंवादे
om śrīmadbhagavadgītāsūpaniṣatsu brahmavidyāyāṁ yogaśāstre śrīkṛṣṇārjunasaṁvāde
भक्तियोगो नाम द्वादशोऽध्यायः श्लोकः ८
bhaktiyogo nāma dvādaśo'dhyāyaḥ ślokaḥ 8

— ॐ —

**मय्येव मन आधत्स्व मयि बुद्धिं निवेशय ।**
**mayyeva mana ādhatsva mayi buddhiṁ niveśaya**
**निवसिष्यसि मय्येव अत ऊर्ध्वं न संशयः ॥१२-८॥**
**nivasiṣyasi mayyeva ata ūrdhvaṁ na saṁśayaḥ** (12-8)

**Therefore with your mind fixed upon my manifest form, let your intellect rest in Me—and thereafter you shall abide in Me alone—of this there is no doubt.** (12.8)

*—: Word-by-Word :—*

**मयि** mayi – in me; **एव** eva – alone; **मनः** manaḥ – mind; **आधत्स्व** ādhatsva – fix; **मयि** mayi – in me; **बुद्धिं** buddhiṁ – intellect; **निवेशय** niveśaya – place; **निवसिष्यसि** nivasiṣyasi – you shall dwell; **मयि** mayi – in me; **एव** eva – alone; **अत** ata – thereafter; **ऊर्ध्वम्** ūrdhvam – henceforth; **न संशयः** na saṁśayaḥ – without a doubt.

*—: Understanding The Verse :—*

— ॐ श्रीकृष्णाय नमः ॐ —

In this verse, Bhagwāna Shri Krishna delivers to Arjuna one of the most direct and luminous instructions of the Gītā. He calls upon Arjuna to fix his mind and intellect solely upon Him, assuring that by so doing, Arjuna will dwell forever in Him without doubt or wavering.

Krishna elevates devotion beyond mere ritual or external practice, drawing us inward toward the heart of divine remembrance and unwavering focus.

It is not enough that the mind alone—which's ever so restless and fickle—be drawn to God; the intellect too, the faculty of discernment and decision, must take its steady refuge in the Divine.

Aye the intellect too must be won—and that's the reason Jnāna too is held so high in Sanātana-Dharma. It is Jnāna which is able to subdue the pure intellect, the voice of reason—and it's for that reason bhakti and Jnāna are considered as the two wings that reach the soul-bird to emancipation.

So deprecate neither—nor take exclusively to one. Have room for both—even though of course, we will always have our favorite companion we like to sit with, depending on our nature—and which is perfectly okay.

— ॐ श्रीरामाय नमः ॐ —

When both the emotional and rational aspects of the being are offered up to the Lord, the seeker transcends the pulls of worldly attachment and realizes his eternal unity with the Supreme.

This verse thus crystallizes the essence of the Gītā's teaching on bhakti as the higher means of spiritual fulfillment—loving absorption in the personal God that leads to abiding in Him both here and beyond—it being an easier path for most of us.

*<u>—: Key Sanskrit Terms :—</u>*

Let us hear the Sanskrit as with steady flame lit in a sheltered room."मय्येव मन आधत्स्व मयि बुद्धिं निवेशय । निवसिष्यसि मय्येव अत ऊर्ध्वं न संशयः ॥ Fix your mind on Me alone, place intellect in Me—you shall live in Me thereafter." Each word burns clear with focused devotion.

Now let us begin by dissecting the key Sanskrit words, through which the verse's intricate layers of meaning come into a sharper focus.

— ॐ —

मय्येव मन आधत्स्व (mayyeva mana ādhatsva):
- मन (manaḥ) — the mind — which is the seat of thought, feeling, and desire,
- आधत्स्व (ādhatsva) — place firmly, fix securely — where?
- मय्येव (mayyeva) — in Me alone.

Here, the Lord commands an exclusive placement of the restless mind wholly upon His being — not divided among worldly concerns, not wavering, but resting entirely in the Divine presence.

— ॐ —

मयि बुद्धिं निवेशय (mayi buddhiṁ niveśaya):
- बुद्धि (buddhi) — the discerning intellect, the faculty of judgment and higher reflection — must also be
- निवेशय (niveśaya) — settled, established — where?
- मयि mayi – in Me, the Lord-God.

Aye, it is not enough that feelings and emotion clings to God, but the higher reason itself, the intellect too must bow, must find its resting-place in the Infinite, free of doubts and arguments.

— ॐ —

निवसिष्यसि मय्येव (nivasiṣyasi mayyeva):

Then, declares Krishna, you shall dwell in:

- मय्येव Me alone — not merely in thought but in being.
- निवास (nivāsa) — dwelling — here indicates a profound identity of existence: no longer the jīva apart from the Divine, but a soul absorbed, resting, established forever in the heart of Braham.

— ॐ —

अत ऊर्ध्वं न संशयः (ata ūrdhvaṁ na saṁśayaḥ):

- अत thereafter, from that point onward,
- ऊर्ध्वम् ūrdhvam, henceforth
- there shall be no न doubt संशयः — no more inner conflict, no more fall into delusion.

The certainty of God-realization, the immovable peace, becomes the soul's unshakeable ground.

## —: *In Brief* :—

— ॐ श्रीकृष्णाय नमः ॐ —

Bhagwāna Shri Krishna now speaks with the authority of one who is both the goal and the guide on the path of liberation: "Fix your mind on Me, and establish your intellect in Me; thereafter you shall surely abide in Me."

The "Me" here encompasses not merely the historical figure of Krishna, but the supreme Puruṣottama—the Lord who pervades all that exists, who dwells within the heart of every being, who is an inexhaustible ocean of compassion, wisdom, sweetness, and joy.

— ॐ श्रीरामाय नमः ॐ —

To fix the mind on Krishna is to turn the restless waves of thought toward the One who alone can still their movements;

To establish the intellect in Him is to anchor all understanding, all discernment, in the profound conviction that the Lord is the highest goal and the ultimate refuge.

But such abiding in God is not merely a matter of philosophical assent or passing emotion—it is the fruit of a life that has learned to withdraw its love from transient things and to pour that love, unreserved and undivided, at the feet of the Supreme Beloved.

The secret of this surrender lies in deep reflection upon the Lord's glories—His leelās, His virtues, His boundless mercy—and in the cultivation of association with those exalted souls who have already made their lives a living sacrifice to Him.

Without such spiritual nourishment, the heart remains caught in the net of worldly enjoyment, unable to taste the sweetness of divine remembrance.

— ॐ अनन्तगुण गम्भीराय नमः ॐ —

Ah what a blessed verse this, because Shri Krishna's assurance here is absolute: there is no doubt **न संशयः** na saṁśayaḥ.

For the one whose mind and intellect are thus absorbed, union with the Divine is not a distant hope, but a living reality.

Yet Krishna also understands the frailty of the human condition, and He anticipates the inevitable question—what of those who struggle to fix their minds and intellects upon Him?

This compassionate anticipation opens the door for the Lord's next teaching, where He tenderly unfolds the graduated means by which all beings, regardless of their starting point, may ascend to His feet.

— ॐ तत सत ॐ —

*Before we move on, let us bow in reverence to this sacred verse. Write it by hand, reflect on its meaning, chant it aloud, make it your own.*

— ॐ —

**मय्येव मन आधत्स्व मयि बुद्धिं निवेशय ।**
**mayyeva mana ādhatsva mayi buddhiṁ niveśaya**
**निवसिष्यसि मय्येव अत ऊर्ध्वं न संशयः ॥१२-८॥**
**nivasiṣyasi mayyeva ata ūrdhvaṁ na saṁśayaḥ (12-8)**

— ॐ —

मय्येव मन आधत्स्व मयि बुद्धिं निवेशय ।
mayyeva mana ādhatsva mayi buddhiṁ niveśaya
निवसिष्यसि मय्येव अत ऊर्ध्वं न संशयः ॥१२-८॥
nivasiṣyasi mayyeva ata ūrdhvaṁ na saṁśayaḥ (12-8)

ॐ तत्सदिति श्रीमद्भगवद्गीतासूपनिषत्सु ब्रह्मविद्यायां योगशास्त्रे श्रीकृष्णार्जुनसंवादे
om tatsaditi śrīmadbhagavadgītāsūpaniṣatsu brahmavidyāyāṁ yogaśāstre śrīkṛṣṇārjunasaṁvāde
भक्तियोगो नाम द्वादशोऽध्यायः श्लोकः ८
bhaktiyogo nāma dvādaśo'dhyāyaḥ ślokaḥ 8

*Om-Tat-Sat—Om (Braham) is the sole Reality. In the Yogic Scripture on the Science-of-Braham, the Shrimada-Bhāgvada-Gītā Upanishad, we hereby conclude Shloka 8 of the Dialogue between Shrī Krishna and Arjuna entitled Bhakti-Yoga, Canto XII*

# ॐ गीता श्लोकः १२.९ – Gītā Verse 12.9

ॐ श्रीमद्भगवद्गीतासूपनिषत्सु ब्रह्मविद्यायां योगशास्त्रे श्रीकृष्णार्जुनसंवादे
om śrīmadbhagavadgītāsūpaniṣatsu brahmavidyāyāṁ yogaśāstre śrīkṛṣṇārjunasaṁvāde
भक्तियोगो नाम द्वादशोऽध्यायः श्लोकः ९
bhaktiyogo nāma dvādaśo'dhyāyaḥ ślokaḥ 9

— ॐ —

**अथ चित्तं समाधातुं न शक्नोषि मयि स्थिरम् ।**
**atha cittaṁ samādhātuṁ na śaknoṣi mayi sthiram**
**अभ्यासयोगेन ततो मामिच्छाप्तुं धनञ्जय ॥१२-९॥**
**abhyāsayogena tato māmicchāptuṁ dhanañjaya** (12-9)

**If however you are unable to fix your mind upon Me steadily, then seek to do so by exercising the Yoga of practice, O Dhananjaya.** (12.9)

*—: Word-by-Word :—*

**अथ** atha – if; **चित्तम्** cittam – mind; **समाधातुम्** samādhātum – to fix; **न** na – not; **शक्नोषि** śaknoṣi – you are able; **मयि** mayi – upon me; **स्थिरम्** sthiram – steadily; **अभ्यास-योगेन** abhyāsa-yogena – by practice of yoga; **ततः** tataḥ – then; **माम्** mām – me; **इच्छाप्तुम्** icchāptum – desiring to attain; **धनञ्जय** dhanañjaya – O Dhananjaya.

*—: Understanding The Verse :—*

— ॐ श्रीकृष्णाय नमः ॐ —

In this verse, Bhagwāna Shri Krishna, embodying infinite compassion, extends His guidance to those who struggle to maintain steady concentration upon Him.

Acknowledging the diverse capacities and temperaments of spiritual seekers, Krishna offers the path of abhyāsa-yoga—the Yoga of repeated practice. For those unable to fix their minds upon the Divine with unwavering firmness, He advises them to cultivate devotion gradually, through continuous effort and gentle redirection of the mind.

— ॐ श्रीरामाय नमः ॐ —

This verse emphasizes that while the ideal of spontaneous, unwavering absorption in the Lord is sublime, the way toward it is accessible to all through patient, diligent practice.

Krishna reveals that the human spiritual journey is not one of perfection from the outset, but of loving perseverance, where each return of the mind to the Divine becomes itself an act of worship and grace—furthering the iteration.

***—: Key Sanskrit Terms :—***

— ॐ तत सत ॐ —

"अथ चित्तं समाधातुं न शक्नोषि मयि स्थिरम् । अभ्यासयोगेन ततो मामिच्छाप्तुं धनञ्जय ॥ If thou cannot fix thy mind steadfast, then strive through practice." With gentle concession, we are asked to step forward with self-possession. Each syllable commiserates with our struggle—bending with compassion.

Let us dwell upon the key Sanskrit terms to unravel the delicate strands of meaning woven into this śloka. But let us not struggle to translate the soul of the verse—just sit besides it; and the Sanskrit, like a companion long silent will begins to speak—not with answers, but with her presence.

— ॐ —

अथ चित्तं समाधातुं न शक्नोषि मयि स्थिरम् (atha cittaṁ samādhātuṁ na śaknoṣi mayi sthiram):

- अथ (atha) — now then, or if it be so — introduces a compassionate concession. If one cannot yet,
- चित्तं समाधातुं (cittaṁ samādhātuṁ) — establish the awareness चित्त in perfect absorption समाध —
- न शक्नोषि (na śaknoṣi) — is not न able to शक्नोषि —
- मयि स्थिरम् (mayi sthiram) — establish स्थिर firmly in Me मयि .

The Lord acknowledges the frailty of the mind — its restless and flickering nature.

And so gently Shri Krishna opens a more accessible way.

— ॐ —

अभ्यासयोगेन (abhyāsayogena):

Through the योग Yoga of अभ्यास Abhyāsa — the Yoga of repeated, disciplined practice.

अभ्यास (abhyāsa) signifies not mechanical repetition, but the patient, loving return of the mind again and again to the Lord, no matter how many times it strays.

अभ्यास is a spiritual cultivation, an inner steadfastness slowly built through loving devotion for the goal.

— ॐ —

माम् इच्छाप्तुम् (mām icchāptum):

- इच्छ (iccha) — long for, desire,
- आप्तुम् (āptum) — to attain Me.

Even the yearning, the sincere wish to reach God through persistent effort, is here praised as a worthy and blessed path.

— ॐ —

धनञ्जय (dhanañjaya):

Krishna addresses Arjuna as धनञ्जय Dhananjaya — conqueror of wealth — a title here laden with subtle meaning: the true wealth to be conquered is the wealth of divine realization, and for that conquest, patience and perseverance are the price.

## *—: In Brief :—*

— ॐ श्रीकृष्णाय नमः ॐ —

Bhagwāna Shri Krishna, in His boundless compassion, speaks not only as the divine instructor of Arjuna but as the eternal friend and guide of all struggling souls. To those unable to sustain a steady, unwavering focus upon Him, Krishna tenderly offers the path of abhyāsa-yoga, the Yoga of repeated practice.

The teaching of the Gītā, though addressed directly to Arjuna, have been resounding across the millenniums, across endless generations, for interminable aspirants—for the Lord knows well the varying dispositions of embodied beings.

Recognizing that few can immediately hold the mind fixed upon the Supreme, Krishna recommends the humble yet mighty discipline of returning the mind again and again to Him.

— ॐ श्रीरामाय नमः ॐ —

अभ्यास Abhyāsa is not mere mechanical repetition, but a holy striving—a conscious, loving effort to recall the Lord's name, form, qualities, and glories.

Whether through visualizing the Lord's resplendent form, meditating upon the sound of the sacred syllable Om, repeating the Divine Names (japa), contemplating the sacred stories and leelās of the Lord, or by stilling the breath and senses through pranayama, the practitioner gradually purifies the mind and awakens the dormant love within the heart.

Just as fire arises from wood when kindled with patience, so too does the Divine Presence reveal itself to the one who perseveres in practice.

— ॐ योगीश्वराय नमः ॐ —

Krishna gently reminds us that the path of practice is not one of haste or discouragement.

Fruits may come swiftly or may ripen slowly, depending upon the aspirant's past impressions, present effort, and the Lord's grace. But regardless of outward signs, no sincere practice is ever wasted; each moment of returning to the Lord chips away at ignorance and deepens the soul's longing for union.

— ॐ खरदूषणसंहारिणे नमः ॐ —

The Lord anticipates the next natural question: What if even the path of practice proves difficult?

Here, Krishna's compassion flows further, as He prepares to outline even simpler methods of approach, showing that there is no soul too fallen or too unsteady to walk toward Him.

Behold O mortal: See how the Gītā reveals itself as a universal scripture—not a doctrine for the few perfected souls, but a divine guide for all seekers who yearn to cross the ocean of manifest existence and rest in the depths of the formless Eternal.

— ॐ तत सत ॐ —

Before moving on, let us once more bow in deep reverence before this sacred verse of the Bhagavad-Gītā, an eternal beacon of wisdom that ceaselessly illumines the path of seekers. Engage with its form—inscribe it with your own hand, let your heart dwell upon its meaning, and raise your voice in its chanting—for within these syllables echoes the undying proclamation delivered millennia ago on the battlefield of Kurukshetra. These words, transmitted unchanged across the unbroken chain of generations, form a living bridge, linking us to that sanctified era when Bhagwāna Shri Krishna Himself walked this earth and bestowed this divine teaching. Through the luminous vibration of these sacred Sanskrit sounds, we are drawn nearer to His timeless presence, touching the very heartbeat of the Eternal.

— ॐ —

**अथ चित्तं समाधातुं न शक्नोषि मयि स्थिरम् ।**
**atha cittaṁ samādhātuṁ na śaknoṣi mayi sthiram**
**अभ्यासयोगेन ततो मामिच्छाप्तुं धनञ्जय ॥१२-९॥**
**abhyāsayogena tato māmicchāptuṁ dhanañjaya (12-9)**

— ॐ —

अथ चित्तं समाधातुं न शक्नोषि मयि स्थिरम् ।
atha cittaṁ samādhātuṁ na śaknoṣi mayi sthiram
अभ्यासयोगेन ततो मामिच्छाप्तुं धनञ्जय ॥ १२-९ ॥
abhyāsayogena tato māmicchāptuṁ dhanañjaya (12-9)

ॐ तत्सदिति श्रीमद्भगवद्गीतासूपनिषत्सु ब्रह्मविद्यायां योगशास्त्रे श्रीकृष्णार्जुनसंवादे
om tatsaditi śrīmadbhagavadgītāsūpaniṣatsu brahmavidyāyāṁ yogaśāstre śrīkṛṣṇārjunasaṁvāde
भक्तियोगो नाम द्वादशोऽध्यायः श्लोकः ९
bhaktiyogo nāma dvādaśo'dhyāyaḥ ślokaḥ 9

**Om-Tat-Sat—Om (Braham) is the sole Reality. In the Yogic Scripture on the Science-of-Braham, the Shrimada-Bhāgvada-Gītā Upanishad, we hereby conclude Shloka 9 of the Dialogue between Shrī Krishna and Arjuna entitled Bhakti-Yoga, Canto XII.**

---

— वेदाङ्गाय नमः —

The Gentle Descent of Grace

"If thou canst fix thy mind in Me, O warrior strong and true,
Then take this lower path of light—I make it near to you."
Thus speaks the Lord not as the God aloof from mortal pace,
But as the friend who bends to lift, with ever-tender grace.

---

He does not scorn the struggling heart, nor shames the failing gaze—
But helps build a stair of soft resolve, and beckons through the haze.
The Gita's voice is low and kind, like mother to her child—
"Begin again, and try once more; the path is steep, not wild."
For where devotion fails, thou may still grow in thy path—
It is अभ्यास abhyāsa, that will now light thy way.

---

The Redemptive Verse Twelve-Nine unveils a profound truth:
Perfection is not demanded. Effort is honored.
Even if the flame of the mind flickers,
Even if Devotion feels dry or distant –
Practice, done sincerely, becomes the path.

---

. Krishna Knows Us Humans

He does not say:
"Be perfect or be gone."
He says:
"If you cannot fix your mind,
Then practice. And practice even more."
The Lord of the World
Does not demand a sage at the very get go.
He invites a student
Willing to stay.

## ॐ गीता श्लोकः १२.१० – GĪTĀ VERSE 12.10

ॐ श्रीमद्भगवद्गीतासूपनिषत्सु ब्रह्मविद्यायां योगशास्त्रे श्रीकृष्णार्जुनसंवादे
om śrīmadbhagavadgītāsūpaniṣatsu brahmavidyāyāṁ yogaśāstre śrīkṛṣṇārjunasaṁvāde
भक्तियोगो नाम द्वादशोऽध्यायः श्लोकः १०
bhaktiyogo nāma dvādaśo'dhyāyaḥ ślokaḥ 10

— ॐ —

**अभ्यासेऽप्यसमर्थोऽसि मत्कर्मपरमो भव ।**
**abhyāse'pyasamartho'si matkarmaparamo bhava**
**मदर्थमपि कर्माणि कुर्वन्सिद्धिमवाप्स्यसि ॥१२-१०॥**
**madarthamapi karmāṇi kurvansiddhimavāpsyasi** (12-10)

**If unequal even to the pursuit of practice, then be resolved to perform the prescribed rites for my sake; surely you shall attain perfection even by performing actions for Me. (12.10)**

### —: *Word-by-Word* :—

**अभ्यासे** abhyāse – in practice; **अपि** api – even; **असमर्थः असि** asamarthaḥ asi – if you are unable; **मत्कर्म-परमः** matkarmaparamah – dedicated to my actions; **भव** bhava – be; **मदर्थम्** madartham – for my sake; **अपि** api – even; **कर्माणि** karmāṇi – actions; **कुर्वन्** kurvan – performing; **सिद्धिम्** siddhim – perfection; **अवाप्स्यसि** avāpsyasi – you shall attain.

### —: *Understanding The Verse* :—

— ॐ श्रीकृष्णाय नमः ॐ —

In this verse, Bhagwāna Shri Krishna, with deep compassion, further lowers the threshold of spiritual practice to embrace even those who struggle with focused meditation or repeated spiritual discipline!

Recognizing that not all seekers possess the same temperament or capacity, Shri Krishna offers the path of selfless action: to dedicate all our works—whether everyday mundane or sacred—as an offering to Him!

By transforming ordinary duties into acts of worship and surrender, the seeker gradually purifies the heart, diminishes the hold of ego, and awakens a consciousness which's attuned to the Supreme.

Krishna assures that even by this very easy path—when pursued with sincerity and without self-interest—the seeker moves toward perfection and ultimate union with Him.

Our Blessed-Lord shows that no one is excluded from the divine embrace; each soul has a path suited to his nature—which leads him steadily toward the same supreme goal.

***—: Key Sanskrit Terms :—***

Let us rest with the Sanskrit as with another handhold being offered to us when we find ourselves short: "अभ्यासेऽप्यसमर्थोऽसि मत्कर्मपरमो भव । मदर्थमपि कर्माणि कुर्वन्सिद्धिमवाप्स्यसि ॥ If not able through practice, then act for My sake, for in acting for Me you will attain perfection." Each word is grounding, practical, direct.

No let us listen not only to what the verse says, but to what it remembers—ancient echoes preserved in Sanskrit syllables, delicate as breath upon a mirror.

— ॐ —

अभ्यासेऽपि असमर्थः असि (abhyāse'pi asamarthaḥ asi):

If you are असमर्थः (asamarthaḥ) — unable, powerless — even in

- अभ्यासे (abhyāse) — in sustained practice, even in the repeated fixing of the mind on the Divine.

Here the Lord, infinitely gentle, acknowledges that even the effort of अभ्यास abhyāsa may prove difficult for some, owing to the turbulence of the mind, the depth of worldly entanglements, or the heaviness of the inner inertia तमस (tāmasic tendencies).

— ॐ —

मत्कर्मपरमः भव (matkarmaparamaḥ bhava):

Then, Krishna says, become wholly devoted to My works —

- मत्कर्म (mat-karma) — actions dedicated to Me, performed for My sake;

- परमः (paramaḥ): holding that alone as the highest aim.

This is the yoga of consecrated action, where the sacredness of life is realized through the spirit of offering all deeds unto the Lord.

— ॐ —

मदर्थम् अपि कर्माणि कुर्वन् (madartham api karmāṇi kurvan):

- कर्माणि कुर्वन् Performing actions, even common actions, but

- मदर्थम् madartham — for the sake of Me – adopting that attitude.

- अपि, api "Even" is significant: even if the action is ordinary, not explicitly spiritual, yet it becomes a means to perfection if its motive and dedication are unto the Divine.

— ॐ —

सिद्धिम् अवाप्स्यसि (siddhim avāpsyasi):

Thus, through the path of humble, devoted action, अवाप्स्यसि one shall attain: सिद्धि (siddhi) — perfection, fulfillment, realization of the true nature of the Self.

—: *In Brief* :—

— ॐ श्रीकृष्णाय नमः ॐ —

Bhagwāna Shri Krishna, ever the compassionate guide, now gently addresses those who find even the path of repeated practice अभ्यास योग (abhyāsa-yoga) difficult to sustain. For such souls, He lovingly prescribes mat-karma—work performed for His sake.

The compound मत्कर्म mat-karma is rich with meaning: it signifies those actions done solely for the Lord, without thought of personal gain, without pride of authorship, and without attachment to the fruits.

Whether one offers service at a temple, provides for family, engages in charity, or fulfills duties large and small, when all is dedicated to the Divine, the ordinary becomes sanctified, and the heart slowly turns Godwards.

— ॐ श्रीरामाय नमः ॐ —

To be "intent on work for Me," as Krishna declares, is not merely to perform religious rituals, but to sanctify all of life. The seeker begins to see every activity as an offering to the Lord—each word, each thought, each deed done for His pleasure.

This spirit of surrender gradually erodes the ego's claims, softens the heart, and prepares the seeker for deeper states of devotion and realization.

Thus Krishna has revealed that the path of karma, when divinized, is no less potent than the path of Dhyāna (meditation) or Gyāna (knowledge).

Importantly, Krishna's teaching reflects the profound inclusiveness of the Gītā: no soul is disqualified from reaching the Supreme. None. Period.

Whether one walks the path of profound contemplation, disciplined practice, or simple selfless service in the cause of Dharma, all roads converge upon the Lord when walked with love and sincerity.

— ॐ कामविजयाय नमः ॐ —

As Krishna unfolds this compassionate vision, He anticipates yet another question: what if even this path of consecrated action proves difficult?

What? Really? Even this easiest of paths would be too difficult for some? Aye—that too is in the realm of possibilities in this world full of wonders.

So true to His boundless mercy, the Lord will next reveal an even gentler path, ensuring that no sincere seeker is left without means of approaching Him.

Ah, the Gītā keeps shining as the most universal scripture, suitable for all —guiding souls at every level toward the blessed shore of divine perfection.

— ॐ तत सत ॐ —

*Before we move on, let us bow in reverence to this sacred verse. Write it by hand, reflect on its meaning, chant it aloud, make it your own.*

— ॐ —

**अभ्यासेऽप्यसमर्थोऽसि मत्कर्मपरमो भव ।**
abhyāse'pyasamartho'si matkarmaparamo bhava
**मदर्थमपि कर्माणि कुर्वन्सिद्धिमवाप्स्यसि ॥१२-१०॥**
madarthamapi karmāṇi kurvansiddhimavāpsyasi (12-10)

अभ्यासेऽप्यसमर्थोऽसि मत्कर्मपरमो भव ।
abhyāse'pyasamartho'si matkarmaparamo bhava
मदर्थमपि कर्माणि कुर्वन्सिद्धिमवाप्स्यसि ॥१२-१०॥
madarthamapi karmāṇi kurvansiddhimavāpsyasi (12-10)

ॐ तत्सदिति श्रीमद्भगवद्गीतासूपनिषत्सु ब्रह्मविद्यायां योगशास्त्रे श्रीकृष्णार्जुनसंवादे
om tatsaditi śrīmadbhagavadgītāsūpaniṣatsu brahmavidyāyāṁ yogaśāstre śrīkṛṣṇārjunasaṁvāde
भक्तियोगो नाम द्वादशोऽध्यायः श्लोकः १०
bhaktiyogo nāma dvādaśo'dhyāyaḥ ślokaḥ 10

Om-Tat-Sat—Om (Braham) is the sole Reality. In the Yogic Scripture on the Science-of-Braham, the Shrimada-Bhāgvada-Gītā Upanishad, we hereby conclude Shloka 10 of the Dialogue between Shrī Krishna and Arjuna entitled Bhakti-Yoga, Canto XII.

— श्रीकृष्णाय नमः —

## A Lower Door Still Open

If thy mind will not in meditation stay,
and the breath of senses run wild, away—then act;
Act not for thy self, but for Me, Krishna—
for the sake of My Sanātana-Dharma I came to reestablish.
Even the hand doth learn to pray—by so doing.
Surely you shall attain perfection by performing Dharmic karmas—
Which I've ordained for thy Varna and Āshram.

# ॐ गीता श्लोकः १२.११ – GĪTĀ VERSE 12.11

ॐ श्रीमद्भगवद्गीतासूपनिषत्सु ब्रह्मविद्यायां योगशास्त्रे श्रीकृष्णार्जुनसंवादे
om śrīmadbhagavadgītāsūpaniṣatsu brahmavidyāyāṁ yogaśāstre śrīkṛṣṇārjunasaṁvāde
भक्तियोगो नाम द्वादशोऽध्यायः श्लोकः ११
bhaktiyogo nāma dvādaśo'dhyāyaḥ ślokaḥ 11

— ॐ —

**अथैतदप्यशक्तोऽसि कर्तुं मद्योगमाश्रितः ।**
**athaitadapyaśakto'si kartuṁ madyogamāśritaḥ**
**सर्वकर्मफलत्यागं ततः कुरु यतात्मवान् ॥ १२-११ ॥**
**sarvakarmaphalatyāgaṁ tataḥ kuru yatātmavān (12-11)**

**And if you are unable to do even that, then simply take refuge in Me, and being self-controlled, renounce the fruits of all actions in Me. (12.11)**

*—: Word-by-Word :—*

**अथ** atha – if; **एतत् अपि** etad api – even this; **अशक्तः असि** aśakto'si – you are unable; **कर्तुम्** kartum – to do; **मद्-योगम्** mad-yogam – devotion to me; **आश्रितः** āśritaḥ – taking refuge in; **सर्व-कर्म-फल-त्यागम्** sarva-karma-phala-tyāgam – renunciation of all fruits of actions; **ततः** tataḥ – then; **कुरु** kuru – do; **यत-आत्मवान्** yatātmavān – with a controlled mind.

*—: Understanding The Verse :—*

— ॐ श्रीकृष्णाय नमः ॐ —

In this verse, Bhagwāna Shri Krishna compassionately offers yet another doorway into the spiritual path, recognizing the diverse temperaments and capacities of seekers.

For those unable to dedicate all their works directly to the Divine or to engage in systematic practice (abhyāsa), Krishna teaches the path of renunciation of the fruits of action—karma-phala-tyāga.

— ॐ जनार्दनाय नमः ॐ —

This path does not demand the complete mastery of the mind or the performance of grand acts of devotion; rather, it asks the aspirant to release attachment to outcomes, to act in the world without craving or fear, and to offer the results inwardly to the Supreme.

By giving up the thirst for reward, the seeker loosens the binding grip of ego and gradually cultivates inner freedom and equanimity. Krishna thus reveals that the very heart of spiritual life is not the outward form of practice, but the inward purification of motive and the relinquishment of selfish desire, leading ultimately to union with the Divine.

*—: Key Sanskrit Terms :—*

Let us hear the Sanskrit as with the doors opened even wider: "अथैतदप्यशक्तोऽसि कर्तुं मद्योगमाश्रितः । सर्वकर्मफलत्यागं ततः कुरु यतात्मवान् ॥ If not able even to act for Me, then renounce all fruits of action, becoming self-controlled." Each syllable unties a knot, making Gītā-Dharma an ever possibility.

Let us illuminate the verse through its key Sanskrit terms, each revealing deeper layers of meaning. Let us read as if the words were written just for us—especially for each one of us. The Sanskrit never closes doors—it opens them – even wider and more easily; and all we have to do is step in restfully, peacefully.

— ॐ —

अथ एतदपि अशक्तः असि (atha etadapi aśaktaḥ asi):
- अथ (atha) — (and) then,
- एतदपि (etadapi) — (of) even this,
- असि (asi) — you are,
- अशक्तः (aśaktaḥ) — incapable, powerless;

The Divine compassion again widens the path: if even the surrender of all actions to the Lord, as described previously, proves too difficult, the soul is still not forsaken.

— ॐ —

मद्योगम् आश्रितः (madyogam āśritaḥ): "Take refuge in My Yoga" — that is, relying upon union with Me, seeking shelter not in one's own strength, but in My grace and guidance.
- आश्रय (āśraya) — refuge — evokes a sacred dependence, a trusting surrender.

— ॐ —

सर्वकर्मफलत्यागं ततः कुरु (sarvakarma-phalatyāgaṁ tataḥ kuru):
- ततः tataḥ Therefore,
- सर्वकर्मफलत्यागं sarva-karma-phala-tyāgaṁ — renounce the fruits of all karmas, and —
- कुरु kuru — do this.

It is not the action itself that need be abandoned, but the craving for its results, the selfish desire for outcomes. Work is performed, but the fruits are given up into the hands of the Supreme.

— ॐ —

यतात्मवान् (yatātmavān):

One who is यतात्मवान् yatātmavān — self-controlled, disciplined, master of the inner impulses.

Even in renouncing fruits, inner steadiness and awareness are essential: the offering must be conscious, not mechanical.

—: *In Brief* :—

— ॐ श्रीकृष्णाय नमः ॐ —

Bhagwāna Shri Krishna, as the most compassionate of teachers, understands the fragile condition of the human soul.

Not every aspirant can yet fix the mind and intellect upon the Divine; not all are prepared to practice sustained meditation or to perform selfless works as offerings to God.

Therefore, Krishna mercifully offers a still more accessible path: a complete surrender and the relinquishment of all the fruits of one's karmas.

— ॐ कर्णामृताय नमः ॐ —

Here the phrase यतात्मवान् yatātmavān—one who has subdued the body, mind, and senses—indicates that even this path does require a foundation of self-mastery, however little it may be.

Without such inner discipline, renunciation of results remains hollow, for the mind, unrestrained, will cling to the rewards of action as its source of identity and satisfaction.

But when the seeker performs duties appropriate to their station in life, renouncing all craving for personal gain, whether in this world or the next, the heart is gradually freed from the tyranny of likes and dislikes, of praise and blame, of success and failure.

— ॐ अच्युताय नमः ॐ —

Philosophically, this verse touches upon the profound principle of nishkāma karma—action without attachment—which was already expounded earlier in the Gītā (notably in chapters 2 and 3) but here is offered as a practical sādhanā leading to God-realization.

This is no mere ethical stance; it is a yogic posture of the soul, which recognizes that the finite self is not the true agent of action. Rather, all acts arise within the cosmic order, guided by the unseen hand of the Divine.

By relinquishing the fruits, the seeker begins to shift the seat of identity from the limited ego to the witnessing Self, which is none other than the indwelling Lord.

— ॐ दामोदराय नमः ॐ —

Importantly, Krishna's teachings here are not hierarchical in the sense of "higher" and "lower" paths, but rather compassionate in their adaptability.

Whether the seeker is drawn to the immediacy of loving surrender, the discipline of repeated practice, the dedication of works, or the relinquishment of fruits, all paths ultimately converge upon the same goal: purification of the heart, dissolution of egoism, and realization of oneness with the Supreme.

What distinguishes these approaches is not the worth of the goal, but the nature of the aspirant's temperament.

— ॐ राघवाय नमः ॐ —

Thus, by tracing out these graduated disciplines, Krishna reveals the vast inclusiveness of the Gītā's vision, leaving no soul without a path to the Divine.

And now anticipating the possibility that people may see karma-phala-tyāga as an inferior way, the Lord, in the next verse, extols the supreme merit of such renunciation, removing all doubts and affirming its spiritual grandeur.

— ॐ तत सत ॐ —

Before we move on, let us bow in reverence to this sacred verse. Write it by hand, reflect on its meaning, chant it aloud, make it your own.

— ॐ —

**अथैतदप्यशक्तोऽसि कर्तुं मद्योगमाश्रितः ।**
**athaitadapyaśakto'si kartuṁ madyogamāśritaḥ**
**सर्वकर्मफलत्यागं ततः कुरु यतात्मवान् ॥ १२-११ ॥**
**sarvakarmaphalatyāgaṁ tataḥ kuru yatātmavān (12-11)**

— ॐ —

अथैतदप्यशक्तोऽसि कर्तुं मद्योगमाश्रितः ।
athaitadapyaśakto'si kartuṁ madyogamāśritaḥ
सर्वकर्मफलत्यागं ततः कुरु यतात्मवान् ॥ १२-११ ॥
sarvakarmaphalatyāgaṁ tataḥ kuru yatātmavān (12-11)

ॐ तत्सदिति श्रीमद्भगवद्गीतासूपनिषत्सु ब्रह्मविद्यायां योगशास्त्रे श्रीकृष्णार्जुनसंवादे
om tatsaditi śrīmadbhagavadgītāsūpaniṣatsu brahmavidyāyāṁ yogaśāstre śrīkṛṣṇārjunasaṁvāde
भक्तियोगो नाम द्वादशोऽध्यायः श्लोकः ११
bhaktiyogo nāma dvādaśo'dhyāyaḥ ślokaḥ 11

Om-Tat-Sat—Om (Braham) is the sole Reality. In the Yogic Scripture on the Science-of-Braham, the Shrimada-Bhāgvada-Gītā Upanishad, we hereby conclude Shloka 11 of the Dialogue between Shrī Krishna and Arjuna entitled Bhakti-Yoga, Canto XII.

## ॐ गीता श्लोकः १२.१२ – Gītā Verse 12.12

ॐ श्रीमद्भगवद्गीतासूपनिषत्सु ब्रह्मविद्यायां योगशास्त्रे श्रीकृष्णार्जुनसंवादे
om śrīmadbhagavadgītāsūpaniṣatsu brahmavidyāyāṁ yogaśāstre śrīkṛṣṇārjunasaṁvāde
भक्तियोगो नाम द्वादशोऽध्यायः श्लोकः १२
bhaktiyogo nāma dvādaśo'dhyāyaḥ ślokaḥ 12

— ॐ —

**श्रेयो हि ज्ञानमभ्यासाज्ज्ञानाद्ध्यानं विशिष्यते ।**
**śreyo hi jñānamabhyāsājjñānāddhyānaṁ viśiṣyate**
**ध्यानात्कर्मफलत्यागस्त्यागाच्छान्तिरनन्तरम् ॥१२-१२॥**
**dhyānātkarmaphalatyāgastyāgācchāntiranantaram (12-12)**

**Compared to mere Practice, Knowledge is far superior; and Meditation is superior even to that. And superior to Meditation is Renunciation of the fruit of actions; and from such Renunciation, there arises immediate peace. (12.12)**

### —: *Word-by-Word* :—

**श्रेयः** śreyaḥ – better; **हि** hi – indeed; **ज्ञानम्** jñānam – knowledge; **अभ्यासात्** abhyāsāt – than practice; **ज्ञानात्** jñānāt – than knowledge; **ध्यानम्** dhyānam – meditation; **विशिष्यते** viśiṣyate – is superior; **ध्यानात्** dhyānāt – than meditation; **कर्म-फल-त्यागः** karma-phala-tyāgaḥ – renunciation of the fruits of actions; **त्यागात्** tyāgāt – from renunciation; **शान्तिः** śāntiḥ – peace; **अनन्तरम्** anantaram – follows immediately.

### —: *Understanding The Verse* :—

— ॐ श्रीकृष्णाय नमः ॐ —

In this verse, Bhagwāna Shri Krishna offers a profound philosophical hierarchy, illuminating the gradations of spiritual practice and their respective capacities to lead the seeker toward liberation and inner peace.

Krishna outlines a progression: from mechanical practice अभ्यास (abhyāsa) to discriminative knowledge ज्ञान (jñāna), from knowledge to meditative absorption ध्यान (dhyāna), and from meditation to the supreme path of renouncing the fruits of action कर्म-फल-त्यागः (karma-phala-tyāga).

By doing so, Krishna reveals not only the relative efficacy of these paths but also the underlying principle that animates them all: freedom from attachment and the purification of the heart.

— ॐ पुण्योदयाय नमः ॐ —

Among these, renunciation of the fruits of action holds a unique power—not only is it the easiest, but it releases the aspirant from the binding forces of ego, desire, and aversion, opening the door to immediate peace (śānti).

This profound verse is not meant to diminish any particular path—but rather to affirm that the culmination of all authentic practice is the relinquishment of self-centered grasping, which alone makes the heart a fit vessel for divine realization.

## *—: Key Sanskrit Terms :—*

Let us linger with the Sanskrit as with scales tipping gently as things are weighed: "श्रेयो हि ज्ञानमभ्यासाज्ज्ञानाद्ध्यानं विशिष्यते । ध्यानात्कर्मफलत्यागस्त्यागाच्छान्तिरनन्तरम् ॥ Knowledge is higher than practice, meditation higher than knowledge, renunciation of fruits higher than meditation — for from that renunciation comes peace." Each word lifts us toward release.

Let us explore the verse. We are not looking through the Sanskrit to find something external. Nay; we are looking with it, looking into it—like one looks into the eyes of a companion and finds, unexpectedly, a reflection of ourselves, or our own longing.

— ॐ —

श्रेयः हि ज्ञानम् अभ्यासात् (śreyaḥ hi jñānam abhyāsāt):
- श्रेयः (śreyaḥ) — greater good, higher blessedness;
- ज्ञानम् (jñānam) — true knowledge, spiritual understanding;
- अभ्यासात् (abhyāsāt) — than mere practice.

Thus, Krishna teaches that knowledge, true insight into the nature of Reality, surpasses mechanical repetition or formal spiritual exercises.

— ॐ —

ज्ञानात् ध्यानं विशिष्यते (jñānāt dhyānaṁ viśiṣyate):
- ध्यानम् (dhyānam) — meditation — surpasses even ज्ञान knowledge;
- विशिष्यते (viśiṣyate) — is distinguished, is superior.

For knowledge that remains intellectual, without inner absorption, is dry and barren. But when knowledge deepens into ध्यान dhyāna, the soul enters direct communion with the Reality it once only understood.

— ॐ —

ध्यानात् कर्मफलत्यागः (dhyānāt karma-phala-tyāgaḥ):

Yet higher than even meditation, Krishna declares, is कर्मफलत्यागः (karma-phala-tyāgaḥ) — the renunciation of the fruits of actions.

For the meditative mind may still harbor subtle desires; but in the pure renunciation of attachment to fruits, the soul becomes truly free, transparent to the Divine Will.

— ॐ —

त्यागात् शान्तिः अनन्तरम् (tyāgāt śāntiḥ anantaram):

From such renunciation त्याग follows peace immediately —

Aye, शान्तिः (śāntiḥ), the still, blissful repose of the soul in Braham, comes अनन्तरम् (anantaram) — without delay.

## —: *In Brief* :—

— ॐ श्रीकृष्णाय नमः ॐ —

Bhagwāna Shri Krishna has lifted the veil upon the inner architecture of spiritual life, revealing a subtle progression of means that lead the soul toward its highest fulfillment.

He declares that mere mechanical practice—whether ritual acts, breath control, or recitation—though useful, remains limited when pursued without discernment or the transformation of the heart.

Knowledge ज्ञानम् (jñāna), the capacity to distinguish the eternal from the ephemeral, spirit from matter, carries the seeker further, for it plants the seed of higher aspiration and clarity.

Yet knowledge, when not ripened into meditative absorption, can remain dry and incomplete, still vulnerable to the pull of the distracted mind.

— ॐ श्रीरामाय नमः ॐ —

Meditation ध्याना (dhyāna) deepens the path, for it is through sustained contemplation upon the Divine—whether formless or with form—that the mind is gradually stilled and the inner world illumined.

But even meditation, Krishna teaches, is surpassed by renunciation of the fruits of action: कर्म-फल-त्याग (karma-phala-tyāga), for it is this inner renunciation that strikes at the very root of bondage: the ego's relentless claim upon action and its results.

Philosophically, Krishna's teaching here pierces to the heart of human suffering. It is not action itself that binds, but the clinging to outcomes, the insistence that "this is mine" or "this must yield me pleasure or recognition."

As long as the fruits of action are claimed by the narrow self, even noble practices can be tainted by subtle desire.

But when the seeker performs action without craving for results, surrendering all into the hands of the Divine, a wondrous transformation takes place—the waves of agitation subside, and the long-sought peace (śānti) dawns, immediate and profound.

— ॐ पुण्यश्रवणकीर्तनाय नमः ॐ —

Krishna's progression does not set the paths in opposition; rather, it shows their culmination.

Practice matures into knowledge, knowledge into meditation, meditation into selfless renunciation—and renunciation blossoms into peace, the ground from which divine realization flowers.

This teaching, so tender and profound, assures the aspirant that the spiritual path is not confined to the ascetic or the scholar; it is open to all, provided one releases the grip of selfish grasping and offers one's life into the vast embrace of the Divine.

— ॐ कुरुक्षेत्रधनञ्जयस्य सारथये नमः ॐ —

Having thus laid out the ladder of practice, Krishna now prepares to describe the luminous marks of the perfected devotee—those rare souls who have realized God and abide in divine love.

It is as though the Lord, having charted the path, now lifts our eyes to the summit, where the realized ones dwell in the radiance of supreme devotion.

— ॐ तत सत ॐ —

Before moving on, let us once more bow in deep reverence before this sacred verse of the Bhagavad-Gītā, an eternal beacon of wisdom that ceaselessly illumines the path of seekers. Engage with its form—inscribe it with your own hand, let your heart dwell upon its meaning, and raise your voice in its chanting—for within these syllables echoes the undying proclamation delivered millennia ago on the battlefield of Kurukshetra. These words, transmitted unchanged across the unbroken chain of generations, form a living bridge, linking us to that sanctified era when Bhagwāna Shri Krishna Himself walked this earth and bestowed this divine teaching. Through the luminous vibration of these sacred Sanskrit sounds, we are drawn nearer to His timeless presence, touching the very heartbeat of the Eternal.

ॐ

**श्रेयो हि ज्ञानमभ्यासाज्ज्ञानाद्ध्यानं विशिष्यते ।**
**śreyo hi jñānamabhyāsājjñānāddhyānaṁ viśiṣyate**
**ध्यानात्कर्मफलत्यागस्त्यागाच्छान्तिरनन्तरम् ॥ १२-१२ ॥**
**dhyānātkarmaphalatyāgastyāgācchāntiranantaram (12-12)**

— ॐ —

श्रेयो हि ज्ञानमभ्यासाज्ज्ञानाद्ध्यानं विशिष्यते ।
śreyo hi jñānamabhyāsājjñānāddhyānaṁ viśiṣyate
ध्यानात्कर्मफलत्यागस्त्यागाच्छान्तिरनन्तरम् ॥ १२-१२ ॥
dhyānātkarmaphalatyāgastyāgācchāntiranantaram (12-12)

ॐ तत्सदिति श्रीमद्भगवद्गीतासूपनिषत्सु ब्रह्मविद्यायां योगशास्त्रे श्रीकृष्णार्जुनसंवादे
om tatsaditi śrīmadbhagavadgītāsūpaniṣatsu brahmavidyāyāṁ yogaśāstre śrīkṛṣṇārjunasaṁvāde
भक्तियोगो नाम द्वादशोऽध्यायः श्लोकः १२
bhaktiyogo nāma dvādaśo'dhyāyaḥ ślokaḥ 12

**Om-Tat-Sat—Om (Braham) is the sole Reality. In the Yogic Scripture on the Science-of-Braham, the Shrimada-Bhāgvada-Gītā Upanishad, we hereby conclude Shloka 12 of the Dialogue between Shrī Krishna and Arjuna entitled Bhakti-Yoga, Canto XII.**

— ॐ जगद्धिताय कृष्णाय गोविंदाय नमो नमः ॐ —

The Ladder of Ascent

The Lord of all hearts speaks to us direct,
Lifting the veil from the inner path.
"Not all reach at once the same height," saith He,
"But all can ascend, step by step, rung by blessed rung."

Abhyasa, practice, is first — the hand repeating what it cannot yet feel,
Even if done mechanically—it matters not initially;
For jñana will soon follow — the lamp of inner discrimination.
And given time, that Jñana will ripen into Dhyana —
That sweet absorption where mind gets in closeness to the Eternal.
But above all—the last, the highest, the quietest step—is:
Inner Renunciation—त्याग *tyaga*—not physically but from the heart.

Practise Without Insight — The Outer Shell

Practise is the first baby-steps;
Be warned: Do not stay content lingering at mere *Abhyasa* all thy life!
O seeker, thou who repeatest prayers in haste,
Who lighteth lamps, yet wandereth in thought —
Know this: Practice alone, without inward flame,
Is like a shell whose pearl is not yet formed.

The fingers move the rosary, the lips recite the Name,
But alas—beneath the noise of rituals, my heart stays asleep.
Yes, do begin there — for movement is the mother of awakening —
Yet seek to awaken within, not merely perform without.
Let thy repetition, thy *Abhyasa*, be the stirring of something deep inside.

Alas, It is a Stairway Few Climb to the Pinnacle

अभ्यास Practice may be low. But is far better than sleep.
ज्ञान Knowledge is high—but is not the summit.
Beyond even wisdom is stillness ध्यान.
Beyond stillness is त्याग tyaga, the letting go from heart.
And only there is Peace शान्तिःशान्तिःशान्तिः

# ॐ गीता श्लोकः १२.१३-१४ – Gītā Verse 12.13-14

ॐ श्रीमद्भगवद्गीतासूपनिषत्सु ब्रह्मविद्यायां योगशास्त्रे श्रीकृष्णार्जुनसंवादे
om śrīmadbhagavadgītāsūpaniṣatsu brahmavidyāyāṁ yogaśāstre śrīkṛṣṇārjunasaṁvāde
भक्तियोगो नाम द्वादशोऽध्यायः श्लोकः १३-१४
bhaktiyogo nāma dvādaśo'dhyāyaḥ ślokaḥ 13-14

— ॐ —

**अद्वेष्टा सर्वभूतानां मैत्रः करुण एव च ।**
**adveṣṭā sarvabhūtānāṁ maitraḥ karuṇa eva ca**
**निर्ममो निरहङ्कारः समदुःखसुखः क्षमी ॥ १२-१३ ॥**
**nirmamo nirahaṅkāraḥ samaduḥkhasukhaḥ kṣamī** (12-13)

**सन्तुष्टः सततं योगी यतात्मा दृढनिश्चयः ।**
**santuṣṭaḥ satataṁ yogī yatātmā dṛḍhaniścayaḥ**
**मय्यर्पितमनोबुद्धिर्यो मद्भक्तः स मे प्रियः ॥ १२-१४ ॥**
**mayyarpitamanobuddhiryo madbhaktaḥ sa me priyaḥ** (12-14)

**He who is friendly and compassionate to all, non-envious, free of the feelings of 'I' and 'mine', balanced in joy and sorrow, forgiving by nature, ever-content, contemplative, self-controlled and of firm resolve, mentally established in Me, who has surrendered his mind and reason to Me—such a devotee of mine is very dear to Me.** (12.13-12.14)

## —: *Word-by-Word* :—

**अद्वेष्टा** adveṣṭā – without hatred; **सर्व-भूतानाम्** sarva-bhūtānām – towards all beings; **मैत्रः** maitraḥ – friendly; **करुणः** karuṇaḥ – compassionate; **एव** ca – and indeed; **निर्ममः** nirmamaḥ – without a sense of ownership; **निरहङ्कारः** nirahaṅkāraḥ – free from ego; **सम-दुःख-सुखः** sama-duḥkha-sukhaḥ – equal in pain and pleasure; **क्षमी** kṣamī – forgiving.

**सन्तुष्टः** santuṣṭaḥ – content; **सततम्** satatam – always; **योगी** yogī – united (in devotion); **यतात्मा** yatātmā – self-controlled; **दृढ-निश्चयः** dṛḍha-niścayaḥ – with firm resolve; **मयि** mayi – in me; **अर्पित-मनोबुद्धि** arpita-manobuddhiḥ – one whose mind and intellect are surrendered; **यः** yaḥ – who; **मद्भक्तः** mad-bhaktaḥ – my devotee; **सः** saḥ – he; **मे** me – to me; **प्रियः** priyaḥ – is dear.

## —: *Understanding The Verse* :—

— ॐ श्रीकृष्णाय नमः ॐ —

In these luminous verses, Bhagwāna Shri Krishna offers a portrait of the perfected devotee—one who is especially dear to Him. Krishna shifts from describing external practices and philosophical disciplines to illuminating the inner virtues that adorn the realized soul.

This devotee is free from malice, abides in universal friendliness and compassion, and has transcended the narrow identifications of "I" and "mine." He remains steady amid life's pleasures and pains, endowed with patience, contentment, and self-mastery. His mind and reason are wholly surrendered to Krishna, and his devotion flows without selfish motive.

These verses provide a profound teaching: that the ultimate measure of spiritual maturity lies not merely in philosophical attainment or ritual observance, but in the refinement of the heart, the dissolution of ego, and the embodiment of divine qualities that mirror the nature of the Lord Himself.

## *—: Key Sanskrit Terms :—*

Let us rest with the Sanskrit as with fragrance filling the air unseen. "अद्वेष्टा सर्वभूतानां मैत्रः करुण एव च । निर्ममो निरहङ्कारः समदुःखसुखः क्षमी ॥... He who hates none, who is friendly, compassionate, free from possessiveness, patient, content, self-controlled, firm in devotion—that one is dear to Me." Each syllable perfumes the heart with qualities of love.

Let us partake of this śloka one golden drop at a time, beginning with the Sanskrit flowers from which its nectar gathers—fragrant, luminous, and slow to bloom. Let us delve into the essence of the verse by carefully examining its pivotal Sanskrit terms.

### *Verse 12.13:*

— ॐ —

अद्वेष्टा सर्वभूतानाम् (adveṣṭā sarvabhūtānām):

One who bears no hatred अद्वेष्टा (adveṣṭā) toward any being सर्वभूतानाम् (sarva-bhūtānām).

This is not mere passive non-hatred, but an active purity of heart, wherein no trace of enmity, resentment, or aversion remains, because the soul sees all beings as expressions of the One.

— ॐ —

मैत्रः करुण एव च (maitraḥ karuṇa eva ca):

- मैत्रः (maitraḥ) — friendly, filled with goodwill toward all;
- करुणः (karuṇaḥ) — compassionate, moved by the suffering of others.

Friendship and compassion become the natural fragrance of the soul that sees unity everywhere.

— ॐ —

निर्ममः निरहङ्कारः (nirmamaḥ nirahaṅkāraḥ):

- निर्ममः (nirmamaḥ) — without possessiveness, the feeling of 'mine';
- निरहङ्कारः (nirahaṅkāraḥ) — free of egotism, the feeling of 'I am the doer.'

Both the sense of ownership and the assertion of personal selfhood are relinquished, and the soul becomes open, vast, and light.

— ॐ —

समदुःखसुखः क्षमी (samaduḥkha-sukhaḥ kṣamī):
- समदुःखसुखः (samaduḥkha-sukhaḥ) — even-minded in pleasure / pain;
- क्षमी (kṣamī) — patient, forgiving.

The waves of duality no longer disturb the inner ocean, and forgiveness flows effortlessly from a heart no longer caught in the thorns of ego.

*Verse 12.14:*

— ॐ —

सन्तुष्टः सततं योगी (santuṣṭaḥ satataṁ yogī):
- सन्तुष्टः (santuṣṭaḥ) — ever content, finding joy within;
- सततं योगी (satataṁ yogī) — continually united with the Divine through inner discipline.

ॐ

यतात्मा दृढनिश्चयः (yatātmā dṛḍha-niścayaḥ):
- यतात्मा (yatātmā) — self-controlled, master of senses and mind;
- दृढनिश्चयः (dṛḍha-niścayaḥ) — of firm and unwavering determination toward the spiritual goal.

— ॐ —

मय्यर्पितमनोबुद्धिः (mayyarpita-mano-buddhiḥ):

He whose मनोबुद्धिः mind and intellect are completely offered अर्पित (arpita) into मयि Me — the full consecration of thought and discernment to the Divine Being.

— ॐ —

यो मद्भक्तः स मे प्रियः (yo mad-bhaktaḥ sa me priyaḥ):

Such a मद्भक्तः mad-bhaktaḥ — My devotee — is most dear - प्रियः (priyaḥ) to मे Me.

Not through grand austerities, not through mere ritual, but through the flowering of these sacred inner qualities does the soul become beloved of the Supreme.

*—: In Brief :—*

— ॐ श्रीकृष्णाय नमः ॐ —

Bhagwāna Shri Krishna, with tender grace, now unveils the characteristics of the devotee who has reached the summit of spiritual realization—one whose very being has become a living temple of divine presence. Such a devotee is अद्वेष्टा सर्व-भूतानाम् adveṣṭā sarva-bhūtānām—free of malice toward all beings.

This freedom from hatred is not born of mere tolerance but of a profound recognition of the One abiding in all, a vision of unity that melts away all tendencies toward enmity.

Flowing naturally from this vision is मैत्रः maitraḥ—friendliness—and करुणः karuṇaḥ—compassion, for the heart steeped in God overflows in spontaneous goodwill and concern for the well-being of all creatures.

— ॐ श्रीरामाय नमः ॐ —

The realized devotee is निर्ममः nirmamaḥ and निरहङ्कारः nirahaṅkāraḥ—free of possessiveness and ego, no longer bound by the narrow walls of "mine" and "I."

Having seen through the illusion of separateness, he lives as an instrument in the hands of the Divine, his sense of authorship dissolved in the great current of God's will.

Amid सुख sukha and दुःख duḥkha—joy and sorrow—he remains सम sama—balanced and serene, for his peace is not anchored in fleeting circumstances but in the unchanging reality of the Self.

— ॐ चिरंजीविने नमः ॐ —

Krishna praises the devotee's क्षमी kṣamī —forgiving nature, which does not merely excuse the faults of others but reflects the deeper understanding that all beings act according to their conditioning and are, like oneself, moving toward the Divine. Such forbearance flows from deep humility and wisdom, not from weakness.

Contentment तुष्टः (tuṣṭaḥ) marks his days—not the transient contentment of worldly fulfillment, but the abiding satisfaction that comes from resting in the inexhaustible bliss of God.

Ever contemplative सततम् योगी (satataṃ yogī), he dwells in constant inward communion, and through steadfast self-mastery यतात्मा (yata-ātmā), he is no longer at the mercy of the senses or whims of the mind. His दृढ-निश्चयः dṛḍha-niścayaḥ—firm resolve—flows from unwavering discernment; having tasted the nectar of the Divine, his intellect no longer wavers before the shifting winds of worldly experience.

— ॐ चतुर्भुजाय नमः ॐ —

Finally, Krishna declares that this devotee has surrendered both mind and reason to Him. This is no mechanical surrender, but the natural culmination of love, where the soul rests wholly in God, not merely as the object of worship but as the sole support and source of its existence.

Such a devotee has offered his entire being into the hands of the Lord and has become transparent to the Divine, shining like a clear flame amid the shadows of the world.

— ॐ अन्जनासुतवन्दिताय नमः ॐ —

In these verses, Krishna reveals that the path to His heart is not merely one of external achievement, intellectual prowess, or ritual precision.

It is the path of inner transformation, where the human heart is refined to mirror the divine heart—radiating love, peace, humility, and equanimity.

Having sketched this sublime ideal, Krishna now prepares to unfold, in the following verses, further qualities that mark the devotee who abides in Him, completing this majestic hymn to the nature of realized love.

— ॐ तत सत ॐ —

**Before we move on, let us bow in reverence to this sacred verse. Write it by hand, reflect on its meaning, chant it aloud, make it your own.**

— ॐ —

**अद्वेष्टा सर्वभूतानां मैत्रः करुण एव च ।**
adveṣṭā sarvabhūtānāṁ maitraḥ karuṇa eva ca
**निर्ममो निरहङ्कारः समदुःखसुखः क्षमी ॥ १२-१३॥**
nirmamo nirahaṅkāraḥ samaduḥkhasukhaḥ kṣamī (12-13)
**सन्तुष्टः सततं योगी यतात्मा दृढनिश्चयः ।**
santuṣṭaḥ satataṁ yogī yatātmā dṛḍhaniścayaḥ
**मय्यर्पितमनोबुद्धिर्यो मद्भक्तः स मे प्रियः ॥ १२-१४॥**
mayyarpitamanobuddhiryo madbhaktaḥ sa me priyaḥ (12-14)

— ॐ —

अद्वेष्टा सर्वभूतानां मैत्रः करुण एव च ।
adveṣṭā sarvabhūtānāṁ maitraḥ karuṇa eva ca
निर्ममो निरहङ्कारः समदुःखसुखः क्षमी ॥ १२-१३ ॥
nirmamo nirahaṅkāraḥ samaduḥkhasukhaḥ kṣamī (12-13)
सन्तुष्टः सततं योगी यतात्मा दृढनिश्चयः ।
santuṣṭaḥ satataṁ yogī yatātmā dṛḍhaniścayaḥ
मय्यर्पितमनोबुद्धिर्यो मद्भक्तः स मे प्रियः ॥ १२-१४ ॥
mayyarpitamanobuddhiryo madbhaktaḥ sa me priyaḥ (12-14)

ॐ तत्सदिति श्रीमद्भगवद्गीतासूपनिषत्सु ब्रह्मविद्यायां योगशास्त्रे श्रीकृष्णार्जुनसंवादे
om tatsaditi śrīmadbhagavadgītāsūpaniṣatsu brahmavidyāyāṁ yogaśāstre śrīkṛṣṇārjunasaṁvāde
भक्तियोगो नाम द्वादशोऽध्यायः श्लोकः १३-१४
bhaktiyogo nāma dvādaśo'dhyāyaḥ ślokaḥ 13-14

**Om-Tat-Sat—Om (Braham) is the sole Reality. In the *Yogic Scripture on the Science-of-Braham, the Shrimada-Bhāgvada-Gītā Upanishad*, we hereby conclude Shloka 13-14 of the Dialogue between Shrī Krishna and Arjuna entitled *Bhakti-Yoga, Canto XII.***

— ॐ योगीश्वराय नमः ॐ —

The Threshold of Divine Portraiture

Now speaketh the Lord not of rites, nor rules,
But of the one who walketh as the Flame —

The realized soul, whose life itself is his temple,
Whose every breath is praise unto Krishna, each movement a veneration.
No crown adorns that soul, no thunder proclaims him,
Yet the Lord declares: This one is dear to Me!

Come, O mortal, climb beyond learning and labor —
Let thy heart be chiselled by these divine lines of Krishna,
For herein is the portraiture of Krishna' very own.

The Heart That Hates No Being

अद्वेष्टा सर्वभूतानां Adveshta sarva-bhutanam — so begins the sacred song,
The heart that hateth none, who casts none aside.
Nay, not tolerance cold, nor kindness feigned,
But the seeing of One in every face—be it man or creature.

O soul, canst thou meet the cow and king alike?
And feel no distance in thy gaze?
He who knows all to be God-wrought,
Cannot favor-unfavor love-hate — for he sees only One, no second,
And of the divine nearness, this is the first gate.

It Ain't Easy—

—For we stay weighed down by this-that, I-other, me-mine.
'Mine' is a chain sunk in the mind, a buried-mine that destructs.
He says 'my, mine'—for house, wealth, deed, body, child, spouse.
But in the end he finds nothing was his—not even breath.

## ॐ गीता श्लोकः १२.१५ – GĪTĀ VERSE 12.15

ॐ श्रीमद्भगवद्गीतासूपनिषत्सु ब्रह्मविद्यायां योगशास्त्रे श्रीकृष्णार्जुनसंवादे
om śrīmadbhagavadgītāsūpaniṣatsu brahmavidyāyāṁ yogaśāstre śrīkṛṣṇārjunasaṁvāde
भक्तियोगो नाम द्वादशोऽध्यायः श्लोकः १५
bhaktiyogo nāma dvādaśo'dhyāyaḥ ślokaḥ 15

— ॐ —

**यस्मान्नोद्विजते लोको लोकान्नोद्विजते च यः ।**
**yasmānnodvijate loko lokānnodvijate ca yaḥ**
**हर्षामर्षभयोद्वेगैर्मुक्तो यः स च मे प्रियः ॥१२-१५॥**
**harṣāmarṣabhayodvegairmukto yaḥ sa ca me priyaḥ** (12-15)

**From whom the world gets no troubles and who gets no troubles from the world; who is free from elation, jealousy, fear, anxiety—such a devotee of mine is dear to Me.** (12.15)

*—: Word-by-Word :—*

यस्मात् yasmāt – by whom; न उद्विजते nodvijate – is not disturbed; लोकः lokaḥ – the world; लोकात् lokaḥ – by whom; न उद्विजते च yaḥ – and who is not disturbed by the world; हर्ष-अमर्ष-भय-उद्वेगैः harṣa-amarṣa-bhaya-udvegaiḥ – from joy, anger, fear, and agitation; मुक्तः muktaḥ – freed; यः yaḥ – who; सः saḥ – he; च ca – and; मे प्रियः me priyaḥ – is dear to me.

*—: Understanding The Verse :—*

— ॐ श्रीकृष्णाय नमः ॐ —

In this verse, Bhagwāna Shri Krishna continues to describe the marks of the devotee who is supremely dear to Him. Here, the Lord shifts focus to the devotee's relationship with the world—a relationship that should be marked by equanimity, harmlessness, fearlessness.

Such a devotee neither becomes a source of disturbance for others nor is disturbed by the world in return. His heart is free from the agitations of elation, envy, fear, and anxiety because his peace is rooted not in outer conditions but in the unshakable presence of God within.

By transcending personal likes and dislikes, such a devotee radiates serenity, becoming a living embodiment of harmony. This verse offers both a description and an ideal: a spiritual mirror into which aspirants can gaze, recognizing the inner dispositions that make one truly beloved of the Lord.

## —: *Key Sanskrit Terms* :—

— ॐ तत सत ॐ —

Let us hear the Sanskrit as with still waters reflecting the infinite sky. "यस्मान्नोद्विजते लोको लोकान्नोद्विजते च यः । हर्षामर्षभयोद्वेगैर्मुक्तो यः स च मे प्रियः ॥ He who disturbs not the world, nor is disturbed by it, who is free from elation, envy, fear, and agitation—he is dear to Me." Each word rests in balance.

Let us draw back the veil of the verse by lingering upon its central Sanskrit expressions, wherein lie the echoes of ancient wisdom and the breath of hidden truths.

— ॐ —

यस्मात् न उद्विजते लोकः (yasmāt na udvijate lokaḥ):
"from whom यस्मात् the world लोकः does not न feel agitation उद्विजते "
The word उद्विजते (udvijate) is rich with implication. It signifies not merely disturbance but an inner trembling, an existential shaking that unsettles one's very composure.

Here, the perfected being becomes like a tranquil lake, whose presence causes no ripple of fear, irritation, or discomfort in others. He stands in such evenness that all who come near him find a natural stillness in their own hearts.

— ॐ —

लोकात् न उद्विजते च यः (lokāt na udvijate ca yaḥ):
"and च who does not न feel agitation उद्विजते from the world लोकात् "
The mutuality here is profound. It is not enough that the sage cause no agitation; he must, in turn, receive none from the world.
The लोक (loka), the world of names and forms, of ceaseless flux, cannot rattle the deep-rooted peace of his being.

Whether praised or insulted, whether caressed by fortune or struck by misfortune, he remains unmoved — untouched, as the lotus in water.

— ॐ —

हर्ष-अमर्ष-भय-उद्वेगैः मुक्तः (harṣa-amarṣa-bhaya-udvegaiḥ muktaḥ):
"freed मुक्त from joy हर्ष, intolerance अमर्ष, fear भय, and anxiety उद्वेग "
Each term unfolds a particular chain that binds the soul:
- हर्ष (harṣa) — the intoxication of elation, the attachment to pleasurable experiences that tightens the knot of संसार saṁsāra.
- अमर्ष (amarṣa) — the fire of resentment and intolerance, the inability to accept the world's ways without personal grievance.

- भय (bhaya) — the primal fear born of duality, the sense of separation from the Eternal.
- उद्वेग (udvega) — the disquietude, the restless upheaval of the mind under the shadow of uncertainty.
- मुक्तः (muktaḥ) — freed, released — signifies not a suppression but a transcending of these states.

It is liberation at the very root of being, where the winds of emotional reaction cannot reach.

— ॐ —

सः च मे प्रियः (saḥ ca me priyaḥ):
"and च such a one सः is dear प्रियः to Me मे "
The sweetness of प्रिय (priya) reveals the Lord's own heart.
It is not cold admiration but intimate, loving acceptance.

This is not merely a moral qualification but a soul-kinship, wherein the bhakta's purified heart resonates harmoniously with the Divine, drawing the Lord's special nearness.

## —: *In Brief* :—

— ॐ श्रीकृष्णाय नमः ॐ —

In this verse, Bhagwāna Shri Krishna here unfolds the subtle beauty of the realized devotee's character—a beauty not measured by outward perfection, but by the inner poise and grace that springs from God-realization.

Such a devotee is described as यस्मान्नोद्विजते लोको yasmat na udvijate lokaḥ, "from whom the world receives no disturbance," and लोकान्नोद्विजते च यः lokaḥ na udvijate ca yasmat, "who is not agitated by the world."

This is no superficial quietness, no mere avoidance of conflict—rather it is the fruit of a heart that has transcended the clamor of ego and rests in the stillness of the Self.

— ॐ श्रीरामाय नमः ॐ —

The realized devotee recognizes the Lord's presence in all beings; therefore, he cannot willfully cause harm, agitation, or fear to any creature.

His life is like a blessing wherever he moves; and his presence radiates peace—like a silent flame casting light without demand.

And when disturbances come to him from the world—when others project anger, envy, or ignorance upon him—he remains undisturbed, not out of cold indifference, but from an unshakable awareness that all events are movements within the vast play of the Divine.

Even when touched by sorrow, he rests in the deep conviction that all is in accordance with a higher order: Shri Krishna knows best.

— ॐ जगन्नाथाय नमः ॐ —

Bhagwāna Shri Krishna further declares that this devotee is free from harṣa (elation) and amara (jealousy), from bhaya (fear) and udvegah (anxiety or mental agitation).

This does not mean that the devotee becomes numb or lifeless; far from it, he is truly alive now than ever, except that his joy is no longer tied to transient acquisitions, nor is his heart darkened when others prosper.

He rejoices in the bliss of the Self. And his sense of self is no longer confined to a narrow "I" but embraces the whole of existence.

Fear and anxiety vanish in that Oneness—because he has surrendered the need to control what is beyond grasp; knowing God as the ground of all existence, he walks the world with a light heart and an unshakable trust in Him.

— ॐ योगेश्वराय नमः ॐ —

Importantly, Krishna's words do not only describe the perfected sage but chart a path for every sincere aspirant.

The Lord's words invite us to examine how often we trouble others with our demands, opinions, or frustrations, and how easily we allow the world to disturb our inner peace.

His words remind us that the true test of devotion is not found in outward piety alone, but in the refinement of the heart: in harmlessness, in cheerfulness over others' success, in freedom from the tyranny of fear.

— ॐ महा योगिने नमः ॐ —

This way Bhagwāna Shri Krishna continues to reveal that devotion is not confined to ritual or isolated meditation, but blossoms most fully in the transformation of one's relationship to life and to all beings.

And having sketched this serene and noble portrait, the Lord will continue to unfold, in the verses ahead, further qualities that shine in the soul illumined by divine love.

— ॐ तत सत ॐ —

Before we move on, let us bow in reverence to this sacred verse. Write it by hand, reflect on its meaning, chant it aloud, make it your own.

— ॐ —

**यस्मान्नोद्विजते लोको लोकान्नोद्विजते च यः ।**
**yasmānnodvijate loko lokānnodvijate ca yaḥ**
**हर्षामर्षभयोद्वेगैर्मुक्तो यः स च मे प्रियः ॥१२-१५॥**
**harṣāmarṣabhayodvegairmukto yaḥ sa ca me priyaḥ (12-15)**

यस्मान्नोद्विजते लोको लोकान्नोद्विजते च यः ।
yasmānnodvijate loko lokānnodvijate ca yaḥ
हर्षामर्षभयोद्वेगैर्मुक्तो यः स च मे प्रियः ॥१२-१५॥
harṣāmarṣabhayodvegairmukto yaḥ sa ca me priyaḥ (12-15)

ॐ तत्सदिति श्रीमद्भगवद्गीतासूपनिषत्सु ब्रह्मविद्यायां योगशास्त्रे श्रीकृष्णार्जुनसंवादे
om tatsaditi śrīmadbhagavadgītāsūpaniṣatsu brahmavidyāyāṁ yogaśāstre śrīkṛṣṇārjunasaṁvāde
भक्तियोगो नाम द्वादशोऽध्यायः श्लोकः १५
bhaktiyogo nāma dvādaśo'dhyāyaḥ ślokaḥ 15

Om-Tat-Sat—Om (Braham) is the sole Reality. In the Yogic Scripture on the Science-of-Braham, the Shrimada-Bhāgvada-Gītā Upanishad, we hereby conclude Shloka 15 of the Dialogue between Shrī Krishna and Arjuna entitled Bhakti-Yoga, Canto XII.

— योगवताराय नमः —

The world disturbs me with every glance—
A slight, a word, and I am undone.

O my heart, so easily wounded, so quick to bleed,
So full of anguish at every imagined injury.

Is this strength—to fall at a person's frown?
Is this devotion—to quake with the shifting winds?

I react as if every ripple were a storm,
As if I were glass—and not the impregnable indestructible soul.

O me, where is thy sanctuary of inner stillness?
Has not the Gita promised—of that unremitting within bliss?

O mind, learn to walk untouched by all this chaos, noise—
let the winds howl, Let the storms pass by
Be like the sky that hosts the storms
But is never shaken by its innumerous thunders contained.

This world will flux and spin. Men will praise or blame—
Why should thee—O child of Eternity—be moved in either case?
Why base thy joy in what they can give or take?

Joyousness is already thine—which bliss never can be taken away.
Be even-minded in gain, in loss,
Taste the sweetness of ceaseless bliss within the Self.

## ॐ गीता श्लोकः १२.१६ – GĪTĀ VERSE 12.16

ॐ श्रीमद्भगवद्गीतासूपनिषत्सु ब्रह्मविद्यायां योगशास्त्रे श्रीकृष्णार्जुनसंवादे
om śrīmadbhagavadgītāsūpaniṣatsu brahmavidyāyāṁ yogaśāstre śrīkṛṣṇārjunasaṁvāde
भक्तियोगो नाम द्वादशोऽध्यायः श्लोकः १६
bhaktiyogo nāma dvādaśo'dhyāyaḥ ślokaḥ 16

— ॐ —

**अनपेक्षः शुचिर्दक्ष उदासीनो गतव्यथः ।**
**anapekṣaḥ śucirdakṣa udāsīno gatavyathaḥ**
**सर्वारम्भपरित्यागी यो मद्भक्तः स मे प्रियः** ॥१२-१६॥
**sarvārambhaparityāgī yo madbhaktaḥ sa me priyaḥ** (12-16)

**Independent, immaculate, adroit, aloof, and untroubled, who renounces the sense of doership in undertakings—such a devotee of mine is dear to Me.**
(12.16)

*—: Word-by-Word :—*

**अनपेक्षः** anapekṣaḥ – free from desires; **शुचिः** śuciḥ – pure; **दक्षः** dakṣaḥ – skillful; **उदासीनः** udāsīnaḥ – indifferent; **गत-व्यथः** gata-vyathaḥ – free from distress; **सर्व-आरम्भ-परित्यागी** sarvārambha-parityāgī – renouncer of all undertakings; **यः** yaḥ – who; **मद्भक्तः** mad-bhaktaḥ – my devotee; **सः** saḥ – he; **मे प्रियः** me priyaḥ – is dear to me.

*—: Understanding The Verse :—*

— ॐ श्रीकृष्णाय नमः ॐ —

In this verse, Bhagwāna Shri Krishna continues to paint the luminous portrait of the devotee who is supremely dear to Him. The Lord extols the virtues of one who is self-sufficient, pure in body and mind, skillful in conduct, impartial in dealings, and undisturbed by life's inevitable ups and downs.

Such a devotee has relinquished the subtle clinging to the sense of authorship, recognizing himself not as the independent doer but as an instrument in the hands of the Divine.

— ॐ श्रीरामाय नमः ॐ —

This verse brings forth the inner disposition of the enlightened soul—one who moves through the world in a state of graceful detachment, radiating purity and balance, free from the tyranny of ego and craving.

Krishna reveals that true spiritual maturity does not lie in the renunciation of action but in the renunciation of the doership behind action, which leads to the flowering of peace, wisdom, and God-intoxicated joy.

*—: Key Sanskrit Terms :—*

— ॐ तत सत ॐ —

Let us linger with the Sanskrit as with mountain air—pure, clear. "अनपेक्षः शुचिर्दक्ष उदासीनो गतव्यथः । सर्वारम्भपरित्यागी यो मद्भक्तः स मे प्रियः ॥ He who is pure, skilled, detached, impartial, content with little, free from restlessness, mind and intellect steady in devotion—he is dear to Me." Each syllable breathes simplicity and clarity.

Now let us listen closely to the verse's ancestral tongue, where each Sanskrit term breathes the air of forgotten heights and cradles meaning like dew upon a lotus.

— ॐ —

अनपेक्षः (anapekṣaḥ): "independent, without expectations"
The word अनपेक्षः (anapekṣaḥ) carries a fragrance of utter freedom.
- Not driven by hopes nor shaken by the lack thereof, the bhakta rests in his own completeness.
- He does not seek favor, recognition, or reward from the world.
- His life flows from an inward abundance, not from thirst or longing.
- He stands like a tree laden with fruit, giving, yet asking nothing in return.

— ॐ —

शुचिः (śuciḥ): "pure, immaculate"
- शुचिः does not refer merely to external cleanliness, but to an inner unsulliedness — the purification of mind and heart.
It denotes clarity free from guile, motives untainted by self-interest, intentions limpid as crystal.
The śuci शुचि soul is a fit vessel for the Divine to dwell within, for in him, the grime of selfishness finds no hold.

— ॐ —

दक्षः (dakṣaḥ): "adroit, skillful"
The bhakta is not inert or negligent.
- दक्षः suggests alertness, competence, a luminous capacity to act rightly in the world.
His actions are not marred by haste or sloth, but executed with graceful precision, rooted in wisdom and detachment.

Skillfulness here reflects the deeper yoga of seamless, natural action, free from egoic interference.

— ॐ —

उदासीनः (udāsīnaḥ): "aloof, impartial"

- उदासीनः depicts a serene detachment, not born of coldness, but of vastness.

The bhakta does not align himself with the currents of partiality — success and failure, gain and loss, approval and blame.

Like the sun, he shines on all without discrimination, untouched by the fleeting tides of worldly dualities.

— ॐ —

गतव्यथः (gatavyathaḥ): "free from distress"

व्यथा (vyathā) refers to the inner agitation born of pain, anxiety, or disillusionment.

To be गतव्यथः is to have crossed the river of sorrow, standing now on the unshakable bank of inner peace.

No outer turmoil can penetrate the citadel of such a heart.

— ॐ —

सर्वारम्भपरित्यागी (sarvārambhaparityāgī): "renouncer of all undertakings (rooted in ego)"

आरम्भ (ārambha) hints at all acts born from the ego's assertion — "I will do," "I will achieve." परित्यागी (parityāgī) signifies the complete relinquishment of this spirit of doership.

It is not the abandonment of necessary action but the quiet renunciation of possessiveness and agency.

Action flows through such a soul without personal claim; he acts, yet is not entangled.

— ॐ —

मद्भक्तः स मे प्रियः (madbhaktaḥ sa me priyaḥ): "such a devotee of Mine is dear to Me"

The sweetness of this refrain returns, a tender echo from the Lord's own heart: that the devotee adorned with these qualities is precious beyond measure — not for what he does, but for what he is.

*—: In Brief :—*

— ॐ श्रीकृष्णाय नमः ॐ —

Bhagwāna Shri Krishna speaks of a devotee who has transcended the restless currents of worldly longing: अनपेक्षः anapekṣaḥ, "one who desires nothing."

This does not imply a dry or lifeless indifference, but rather a heart so filled with the sweetness of the Divine that nothing external has power over it. Such a soul no longer acts under the compulsion of personal craving; whatever arises in life—whether pleasure or pain, success or loss—is accepted as the unfolding of the Divine will.

— ॐ श्रीरामाय नमः ॐ —

This devotee is शुचिः śuciḥ, pure—both outwardly in conduct and inwardly in heart.

His purity is not merely ritual, but existential: his thoughts, intentions, and actions are free from the stains of selfishness, deceit, or malice.

By his mere presence, the atmosphere around him becomes sanctified; the earth upon which he walks, the water he touches, and the hearts he encounters are uplifted and illumined.

— ॐ चक्रपाणये नमः ॐ —

Krishna praises him as दक्षः dakṣaḥ, skillful—not necessarily in worldly arts or commerce, but in the supreme art of living, the art of aligning all thought and action with the goal of God-realization.

True cleverness, as the Lord gently teaches, is not measured by worldly achievements but by success in attaining the purpose for which human birth was granted: the realization of the Self.

उदासीन udāsīnaḥ, the devotee remains aloof—not cold or withdrawn, but serenely detached, unentangled in the waves of partiality or passion. In dealings with others, he is गतव्यथः gatavyathaḥ, undisturbed, free of anxiety or sorrow, even when faced with loss or misfortune.

Such equipoise arises not from emotional numbness but from deep surrender: the recognition that all events are part of the cosmic play of Māyā, and that the egoic sense of control is a veil over the deeper truth.

— ॐ वामनाय नमः ॐ —

Most profound is his renunciation of सर्वारम्भपरित्यागी sarvārambha-parityāgī—the abandonment of the feeling of doership.

Though outwardly engaged in action, the enlightened devotee no longer claims authorship or merit.

He understands himself to be a mere instrument निमित्त (nimitta) in the hands of the Lord, gladly fulfilling whatever role the Divine assigns, free of the inner bondage of ego.

This is the highest form of renunciation, for it severs the root of suffering—the illusion: that "I am the doer" and "these results are mine."

— ॐ सीतासहायाय नमः ॐ —

In this verse, Krishna thus reveals a path that transcends mere ritual, intellectual knowledge, or even isolated meditation.

It is the transformation of the heart and the radical surrender of ego that draw the soul into the intimate embrace of the Divine.

And having unfolded this vision, Krishna continues to describe further qualities of the devotee in the upcoming verses—weaving a tapestry of love, wisdom, and freedom that points the way to man's ultimate union with the divine.

— ॐ तत सत ॐ —

Before we move on, let us bow in reverence to this sacred verse. Write it by hand, reflect on its meaning, chant it aloud, make it your own.

— ॐ —

**अनपेक्षः शुचिर्दक्ष उदासीनो गतव्यथः ।**
**anapekṣaḥ śucirdakṣa udāsīno gatavyathaḥ**
**सर्वारम्भपरित्यागी यो मद्भक्तः स मे प्रियः ॥१२-१६॥**
**sarvārambhaparityāgī yo madbhaktaḥ sa me priyaḥ (12-16)**

अनपेक्षः शुचिर्दक्ष उदासीनो गतव्यथः ।
anapekṣaḥ śucirdakṣa udāsīno gatavyathaḥ
सर्वारम्भपरित्यागी यो मद्भक्तः स मे प्रियः ॥१२-१६॥
sarvārambhaparityāgī yo madbhaktaḥ sa me priyaḥ (12-16)

ॐ तत्सदिति श्रीमद्भगवद्गीतासूपनिषत्सु ब्रह्मविद्यायां योगशास्त्रे श्रीकृष्णार्जुनसंवादे
om tatsaditi śrīmadbhagavadgītāsūpaniṣatsu brahmavidyāyāṁ yogaśāstre śrīkṛṣṇārjunasaṁvāde
भक्तियोगो नाम द्वादशोऽध्यायः श्लोकः १६
bhaktiyogo nāma dvādaśo'dhyāyaḥ ślokaḥ 16

Om-Tat-Sat—Om (Braham) is the sole Reality. In the Yogic Scripture on the Science-of-Braham, the Shrimada-Bhāgvada-Gītā Upanishad, we hereby conclude Shloka 16 of the Dialogue between Shrī Krishna and Arjuna entitled Bhakti-Yoga, Canto XII.

— ॐ —

He leans on naught, not praise nor passing gold,
Nor friend's delight, nor foe's retort grown bold.
Not hungry-eyed for gestures, gifts, fame, name—
He stands apart from want and worldly games.

As lotus leaf upon the water lies,
Yet takes no stain, though wet beneath the skies—
So he doth walk amidst both feast and fray,
Yet draws no need from night, nor light of day.

Independent, immaculate, adroit, aloof, untroubled by the play of senses,
*Anapekṣaḥ* अनपेक्षः he stays—one whose root is deep within his Self.

# ॐ गीता श्लोकः १२.१७ – GĪTĀ VERSE 12.17

ॐ श्रीमद्भगवद्गीतासूपनिषत्सु ब्रह्मविद्यायां योगशास्त्रे श्रीकृष्णार्जुनसंवादे
om śrīmadbhagavadgītāsūpaniṣatsu brahmavidyāyāṁ yogaśāstre śrīkṛṣṇārjunasaṁvāde
भक्तियोगो नाम द्वादशोऽध्यायः श्लोकः १७
bhaktiyogo nāma dvādaśo'dhyāyaḥ ślokaḥ 17

— ॐ —

**यो न हृष्यति न द्वेष्टि न शोचति न काङ्क्षति ।**
**yo na hṛṣyati na dveṣṭi na śocati na kāṅkṣati**
**शुभाशुभपरित्यागी भक्तिमान्यः स मे प्रियः** ॥१२-१७॥
**śubhāśubhaparityāgī bhaktimānyaḥ sa me priyaḥ** (12-17)

**He who neither rejoices nor detests, nor grieves, nor desires; having renounced both good and evil who is full of devotion—such a devotee is dear to Me.** (12.17)

*—: Word-by-Word :—*

**यो** yaḥ – who; **न हृष्यति** na hṛṣyati – neither rejoices; **न द्वेष्टि** na dveṣṭi – nor hates; **न शोचति** na śocati – nor grieves; **न काङ्क्षति** na kāṅkṣati – nor desires; **शुभ-अशुभ-परित्यागी** śubha-aśubha-parityāgī – renouncer of good and bad; **भक्तिमान्** bhaktimān – full of devotion; **यः** yaḥ – who; **सः** saḥ – he; **मे प्रियः** me priyaḥ – is dear to me.

*—: Understanding The Verse :—*

— ॐ श्रीकृष्णाय नमः ॐ —

In this verse, Bhagwāna Shri Krishna unfolds another precious facet of the qualities that make a devotee supremely dear to Him. Here, the Lord praises the devotee who has transcended the turbulent oscillations of worldly emotion—the fluctuations of joy and sorrow, attraction and aversion, desire and grief.

This devotee stands firm in equanimity, having relinquished attachment even to the distinction between "good" and "evil" deeds—for his heart is now anchored solely in the Divine.

Such a one perceives all events as expressions of God's will and remains untouched by the shifting tides of fortune and adversity.

— ॐ श्रीरामाय नमः ॐ —

Krishna reveals that this serenity is not a withdrawal from life but a profound immersion in the bliss of divine realization, where the world is no longer a realm of gain or loss but a living expression of the Beloved. It is this freedom of heart, adorned with unwavering devotion, that draws the soul closest to God.

## —: Key Sanskrit Terms :—

— ॐ तत सत ॐ —

Let us rest with the Sanskrit as with flame untroubled by gusts. "यो न हृष्यति न द्वेष्टि न शोचति न काङ्क्षति । शुभाशुभपरित्यागी भक्तिमान्यः स मे प्रियः ॥ He who neither rejoices nor hates, who grieves not nor desires, who renounces both good and evil—he is dear to Me." Each word steadies the heart beyond dualities.

Now let us lean in as one leans toward a flame in a darkened room—not to deplete it, but to see more clearly. The Sanskrit terms flicker here steady and ancient, casting long shadows of meaning across the walls of our awareness. Let us trace the contours of these meanings focusing on the pivotal Sanskrit terms which quietly illuminate our path.

— ॐ —

यो न हृष्यति (yo na hṛṣyati): "who does not rejoice"

The term हृष्यति (hṛṣyati) speaks of outward elation, the bubbling of joy when fortune smiles.

Yet this joy, bound to circumstances, remains fragile and fleeting.

The sage is unmoved by such outer pleasures, for his joy is not borrowed from the world; it wells up from the imperishable Self within.

His heart neither inflates with success nor collapses with failure.

— ॐ —

न द्वेष्टि (na dveṣṭi): "does not hate"

- द्वेष (dveṣa) is aversion born of the perception of threat, competition, or injury.

The perfected being sees all as manifestations of the Divine play — the agreeable and the disagreeable alike. Thus he harbors no enmity, for he perceives no true "other" against whom hatred could arise.

— ॐ —

न शोचति (na śocati): "does not grieve"

- शोचति (śocati), grief, arises from loss — the clinging of the heart to that which is impermanent.

Yet the one who has discerned the eternal knows that nothing real can be lost, and nothing unreal was ever truly possessed.

In this deep seeing, grief evaporates like mist before the sun.

— ॐ —

न काङ्क्षति (na kāṅkṣati): "does not desire"

- काङ्क्षति (kāṅkṣati) points to the restless longing that binds the soul to saṁsāra.

Desire begets agitation; agitation clouds wisdom. But he who dwells in the completeness of the Self seeks nothing outside himself; he has no hunger, for he knows himself as fullness itself.

— ॐ —

शुभाशुभपरित्यागी (śubhāśubhaparityāgī): "renouncer of both good and evil"

Profound is this teaching. शुभ (śubha) and अशुभ (aśubha) — good and evil — belong to the realm of relative morality, which binds even the virtuous to the wheel of birth and death.

The परित्यागी (parityāgī) transcends this duality, offering all actions into the fire of knowledge, seeing no independent reality in either merit or demerit.

— ॐ —

भक्तिमान् (bhaktimān): "endowed with devotion"

In the midst of detachment, it is भक्ति bhakti — tender, unwavering love for the Supreme — that enlivens the heart.

This is no dry renunciation but a flowering of the soul toward its Divine Source.

— ॐ —

यः स मे प्रियः (yaḥ sa me priyaḥ): "such a one is dear to Me"

The Lord's love for such a soul is not a favor granted but a natural recognition — as the river naturally rushes to the ocean, so the Lord embraces the bhakta whose heart is emptied of the finite and filled with the Infinite.

## —: In Brief :—

— ॐ श्रीकृष्णाय नमः ॐ —

Bhagwāna Shri Krishna illuminates here the heart of the devotee who neither rejoices nor hates, neither grieves nor craves, and who has renounced both auspicious and inauspicious deeds. This is no ordinary emotional detachment but the flowering of the soul that has tasted the supreme sweetness of God within himself.

— ॐ श्रीरामाय नमः ॐ —

यो न हृष्यति न द्वेष्टि yo na hṛṣyati na dveṣṭi—he neither rejoices nor hates. While ordinary beings are tossed by waves of joy at the attainment of desires and bitterness when faced with aversion, the enlightened devotee abides in a joy beyond objects.

His love is anchored in the all-pervading Lord, who alone is the true source of bliss. To such a one, the transient play of worldly circumstances no longer holds the power to elate or embitter.

— ॐ जगदेकधारिणे नमः ॐ —

न शोचति न काङ्क्षति na śocati na kāṅkṣati—he neither grieves nor craves. The world teaches us to grieve for loss and hunger for gain. But the devotee who dwells in God sees all gains and losses as waves in the ocean of divine play.

He knows no separation from his Beloved; thus, how can there be grief? And having discovered the fountain of fulfillment within, how can there be craving for perishable things?

— ॐ मुकुन्दाय नमः ॐ —

शुभाशुभपरित्यागी śubha-aśubha-parityāgī—he has relinquished both good and evil actions.

This does not mean he has become indifferent to virtue or abandoned dharma; rather, he has offered all actions, noble and ordinary, at the feet of the Lord.

He acts without attachment, without the sense of "I am the doer" or "this is mine."

His good deeds no longer carry the seed of pride, nor do they bind him with expectation of reward; likewise, free of selfish grasping, he does not slip into wrong action.

Having surrendered the sense of agency, his very life becomes a silent offering to the Lord-God—sanctified and purified.

— ॐ युगाधिपाय नमः ॐ —

भक्तिमान Bhaktimān—he is full of devotion. It is devotion alone that transforms this state from lifeless indifference into living surrender.

Without devotion, detachment can become dry, even harsh. But in the devotee, detachment is softened and illumined by love; it becomes a spacious, luminous freedom in which the soul, unburdened, rests joyfully in God.

— ॐ पितृ भक्ताय नमः ॐ —

Krishna's description is not merely a distant ideal but a living invitation. It calls the seeker to examine the restless pendulum of his own mind—the pulls of pleasure and pain, attachment and aversion—and to gradually wean the heart from its outward grasping, turning it inward toward the inexhaustible wellspring of divine joy.

As Krishna continues further, He will offer yet deeper glimpses into the nature of the beloved devotee, drawing the attentive listener into the very heart of divine love.

— ॐ तत सत ॐ —

Before we move on, let us bow in reverence to this sacred verse. Write it by hand, reflect on its meaning, chant it aloud, make it your own.

— ॐ —

**यो न हृष्यति न द्वेष्टि न शोचति न काङ्क्षति ।**
yo na hṛṣyati na dveṣṭi na śocati na kāṅkṣati
**शुभाशुभपरित्यागी भक्तिमान्यः स मे प्रियः ॥१२-१७॥**
śubhāśubhaparityāgī bhaktimānyaḥ sa me priyaḥ (12-17)

यो न हृष्यति न द्वेष्टि न शोचति न काङ्क्षति ।
yo na hṛṣyati na dveṣṭi na śocati na kāṅkṣati
शुभाशुभपरित्यागी भक्तिमान्यः स मे प्रियः ॥१२-१७॥
śubhāśubhaparityāgī bhaktimānyaḥ sa me priyaḥ (12-17)

ॐ तत्सदिति श्रीमद्भगवद्गीतासूपनिषत्सु ब्रह्मविद्यायां योगशास्त्रे श्रीकृष्णार्जुनसंवादे
om tatsaditi śrīmadbhagavadgītāsūpaniṣatsu brahmavidyāyāṁ yogaśāstre śrīkṛṣṇārjunasaṁvāde
भक्तियोगो नाम द्वादशोऽध्यायः श्लोकः १७
bhaktiyogo nāma dvādaśo'dhyāyaḥ ślokaḥ 17

Om-Tat-Sat—Om (Braham) is the sole Reality. In the Yogic Scripture on the Science-of-Braham, the Shrimada-Bhāgvada-Gītā Upanishad, we hereby conclude Shloka 17 of the Dialogue between Shrī Krishna and Arjuna entitled Bhakti-Yoga, Canto XII.

— ॐ ईश्वराय नमः ॐ —

Beyond the Whirl of Joy and Grief

He who does not leap with joy nor fall to sorrow's floor,
Who walks through weal and woe alike, and clings to neither shore—
Such is the soul that Krishna names, with voice of sweetest hush,
As dearer than a thousand prayers,
More fragrant than the morning lotus blush—
near banks where Yamuna softly murmurs.

For he has left the rise and fall of mortal things.
No gladness makes his chest expand, nor grief does crush his frame,
He stands in flames, yet stays unburnt—unmoved by praise and blame.
This is the Karma-Yogi Krishna loves to see
—beyond name, fame, fruits, claims—
who rejoices nor detests, nor grieves, nor desires,
so has renounced both good and evil—
staying in the fullness of bliss — performing his Varna-Âshram Dharma.

## ॐ गीता श्लोकः १२.१८-१९ – GĪTĀ VERSE 12.18-19

ॐ श्रीमद्भगवद्गीतासूपनिषत्सु ब्रह्मविद्यायां योगशास्त्रे श्रीकृष्णार्जुनसंवादे
om śrīmadbhagavadgītāsūpaniṣatsu brahmavidyāyāṁ yogaśāstre śrīkṛṣṇārjunasaṁvāde
भक्तियोगो नाम द्वादशोऽध्यायः श्लोकः १८-१९
bhaktiyogo nāma dvādaśo'dhyāyaḥ ślokaḥ 18-19

— ॐ —

**समः शत्रौ च मित्रे च तथा मानापमानयोः ।**
**samaḥ śatrau ca mitre ca tathā mānāpamānayoḥ**
**शीतोष्णसुखदुःखेषु समः सङ्गविवर्जितः ॥१२-१८॥**
**śītoṣṇasukhaduḥkheṣu samaḥ saṅgavivarjitaḥ** (12-18)

**तुल्यनिन्दास्तुतिर्मौनी सन्तुष्टो येन केनचित् ।**
**tulyanindāstutirmaunī santuṣṭo yena kenacit**
**अनिकेतः स्थिरमतिर्भक्तिमान्मे प्रियो नरः ॥१२-१९॥**
**aniketaḥ sthiramatirbhaktimānme priyo naraḥ** (12-19)

**Free of attachments; alike to friend and foe; the same in honor and disgrace; equanimous in joy, sorrow, heat, cold and such pairs of dualities; reticent; he who takes praise and reproach alike; who is content with any available means of subsistence; who entertains no sense of ownership or attachment with respect to the dwelling place; who is given to contemplation; and is of unflinching steady mind—such a devotee of mine is dear to Me.** (12.18-12.19)

*—: Word-by-Word :—*

समः samaḥ – equal; शत्रौ śatrau – towards enemy; च ca – and; मित्रे mitre – friend; च ca – and; तथा tathā – likewise; मान-अपमानयोः māna-apamānayoḥ – in honor and dishonor; शीत-उष्ण-सुख-दुःखेषु śīta-uṣṇa-sukha-duḥkheṣu – in cold, heat, pleasure, and pain; समः samaḥ – even-minded; सङ्ग-विवर्जितः saṅga-vivarjitaḥ – free from attachment.

तुल्य-निन्दा-स्तुतिः tulya-nindā-stutiḥ – equal in praise and blame; मौनी maunī – silent (self-restrained in speech); सन्तुष्टः santuṣṭaḥ – content; येन केनचित् yena kenacit – with anything; अनिकेतः aniketaḥ – without a fixed abode; स्थिर-मतिः sthira-matiḥ – steady-minded; भक्तिमान् bhaktimān – full of devotion; मे me – to me; प्रियः priyaḥ – dear; नरः naraḥ – the person.

*—: Understanding The Verse :—*

— ॐ श्रीकृष्णाय नमः ॐ —

*Verse 12.18*

In this verse Bhagwāna Shri Krishna deepens His portrayal of the qualities cherished in the heart of the perfect devotee. Krishna presents here a portrait of equanimity that transcends all dualities and opposites of the worldly plane—friend and foe, honor and dishonor, pleasure and pain, heat and cold.

The ideal devotee stands unmoved, not because he is numb or indifferent, but because his heart rests in the unwavering presence of the Divine, whose play is seen in all things.

Such a soul does not collapse into favoritism or aversion, nor is his peace broken by praise or blame.

He perceives all beings and all experiences as arising from the same divine source, and thus moves through the world untouched by personal attachments, standing in a state of inner freedom and serene balance.

This verse invites us aspirants to contemplate the profound power of non-attachment—not as cold withdrawal, but as the flowering of universal love free of possessiveness.

— ॐ श्रीरामाय नमः ॐ —

*Verse 12.19*

Here Bhagwāna Shri Krishna further unveils the sublime character of the perfected devotee—the one who has crossed beyond the opposites of worldly experience and rests unwavering in the Divine.

This devotee meets praise and blame with equal serenity, remains absorbed in contemplation, is content with whatever destiny brings, and lives without possessiveness or attachment, even toward his dwelling place.

Such a soul is no longer driven by the restless mind or outward identifications but has become a silent, steady flame of devotion.

Krishna thus points to the interior renunciation that marks the highest stage of bhakti—not merely the renunciation of objects, but the abandonment of self-claim over them, coupled with deep contentment in the Beloved.

These verses beautifully weave together the essence of freedom, simplicity, and surrender, describing a life wholly consecrated to the Divine—and which will one day take him to oneness in Him. For that is the whole idea of the Bhagavad-Gitā: for us to become one in the Divine, which is our very own nature!

*—: Key Sanskrit Terms :—*

Let us touch the Sanskrit as with gems unyielding, smooth, silent. "समः शत्रौ च मित्रे च तथा मानापमानयोः । शीतोष्णसुखदुःखेषु समः सङ्गविवर्जितः ॥... Alike to friend and foe, to honor and dishonor, to heat and cold, to joy and sorrow, to praise and blame; silent, content, firm in resolve, mind devoted—he is dear to Me." Each syllable shapes equanimity into veneration.

Let us remain within the living hush of the verses, held steady by their Sanskrit expressions—ancient, tender, and slowly rendering life into ambrosia. Ah, we can never thank Arjuna and Krishna enough for bringing within our reach this divine nectar called the Bhagavad-Gītā!

---

*Verse 12.18*

— ॐ —

समः शत्रौ च मित्रे च (samaḥ śatrau ca mitre ca): "equal to enemy and friend"
- समः (samaḥ) — sameness — is the crown of spiritual maturity.
To see alike both
- शत्रु (śatru), the adversary, and
- मित्र (mitra), the well-wisher, is not the dulling of the heart but the flowering of true vision.

Recognizing the Self in all beings, the sage does not discriminate in his inner regard, whether met with hostility or affection.

---

— ॐ —

मानापमानयोः समः (mānāpamānayoḥ samaḥ): "equanimous in honor and dishonor"
- मान (māna) — honor, and
- अपमान (apamāna) — dishonor — are but reflections in the mirror of the world.

The wise, knowing themselves not to be the reflected image but the unchanging light, remain untouched by both. Neither praise inflates them nor insult deflates them.

---

— ॐ —

शीतोष्णसुखदुःखेषु समः (śītoṣṇasukhaduḥkheṣu samaḥ): "equanimous in cold and heat, pleasure and pain"

The sage is as the mountain that remains unmoved by the passing seasons.

शीत (śīta) — cold; उष्ण (uṣṇa) — heat; सुख (sukha) — pleasure; दुःख (duḥkha) — pain — all come and go like waves.

The स्थित-प्रज्ञ sthita-prajña dwells in the heart of all seasons, witnessing their play without inner disturbance.

---

— ॐ —

सङ्गविवर्जितः (saṅgavivarjitaḥ): "free from attachment"
- सङ्ग (saṅga) — attachment — binds the soul to sorrow.

To be विवर्जित (vivarjita) of सङ्ग saṅga is to live amidst the world without sinking into it, to touch life fully without clinging.

*Verse 12.19*

— ॐ —

तुल्यनिन्दास्तुतिः (tulyanindāstutiḥ): "equal in censure and praise"
Whether subjected to
- निन्दा (nindā) — slander — or
- स्तुति (stuti) — glorification — the sage remains undisturbed, equanimous तुल्य.
He does not build his identity upon the unstable sands of others' opinions.

— ॐ —

मौनी (maunī): "silent"
- मौन (mauna) is not merely the absence of speech but the flowering of inner stillness.
It is the silence that springs from understanding, where speech arises only as needed, imbued with truth and compassion.

— ॐ —

सन्तुष्टः येन केनचित् (santuṣṭaḥ yena kenacit): "content with whatever comes"
- सन्तोष (santoṣa) — contentment — is the ornament of the sage.
Whatever provision destiny places before him, he accepts without complaint or craving, knowing that true sustenance lies in the Self, not in external forms.

— ॐ —

अनिकेतः (aniketaḥ): "without fixed abode"
- निकेत (niketa) suggests the fixed habitation of attachment.
- अनिकेत (aniketa) reveals the one who regards no place, no position, no possession as his own.
His true home is the boundless Self—infinite, unconfined.

— ॐ —

स्थिरमति (sthiramatiḥ): "steady of mind"
- स्थिर (sthira) means firm, unmoving;
- मति (mati) is the understanding or intellect.
To be स्थिरमति is to hold unwaveringly to the truth of the Self, unaffected by the tremors of the external world.

— ॐ —

भक्तिमान् (bhaktimān): "endowed with devotion"

And ever the essence — भक्ति (bhakti) — pure, unwavering devotion, binds all these virtues in a single garland offered at the Lord's feet.

— ॐ —

**समे प्रियः** (sa me priyaḥ): "such a one is dear to Me"

The Lord affirms again His intimate love for the soul that wears these qualities as his very nature — not as mere discipline, but as a spontaneous expression of realized being.

## *—: In Brief :—*

— ॐ श्रीकृष्णाय नमः ॐ —

*Verse 12.18*

Bhagwāna Shri Krishna here unveils the quiet majesty of the devotee who has transcended the stormy waves of duality.

Such a devotee, **समः शत्रौ च मित्रे च** samaḥ śatrau ca mitre ca—alike to friend and foe—does not live in a world divided by the sharp lines of favoritism or enmity.

While ordinary minds are easily stirred by affection toward those who please them and resentment toward those who oppose them, the realized devotee sees beyond these surface distinctions.

Just as the sun shines impartially upon all, so does the heart of the devotee radiate love and goodwill without discrimination, seeing the hand of the Divine in every being and circumstance.

— ॐ सीतापतये नमः ॐ —

Be warned: Seeing oneness in all—enemy or friend—because all existence is the one being: satt-chitt-ānanda braham, does not imply blanket forgiveness.

As Krishna has told Arjuna repeatedly in the Gitā: slay these enemies-of-Dharma that stand before—because that is your duty; or else Dharma itself will become destroyed, and the garden of dharma which has sustained humanity thus long, will become a wilderness with just adharmika beasts ruling the roost—as is happening at the present time.

The vision of oneness helps us to rise above our personal feelings and stay aloof—but we still stay guided by the dictates of Sanātana-Dharma, that have been so clearly spelled out in Manu-smriti, Mahabharata etc., the many scriptures of Sanātana-Dharma.

— ॐ श्रीरामाय नमः ॐ —

तथा मानापमानयोः tathā māna-apamānayoḥ—equally balanced in honor and dishonor.

Whether praised or blamed, lifted up or cast down in the eyes of the world, the devotee remains steady, for his worth is no longer measured by the fleeting judgments of men but by his intimate union with the Supreme.

शीतोष्णसुखदुःखेषु śītoṣṇa-sukha-duḥkheṣu—in heat and cold, pleasure and pain, and all the fluctuating conditions of life, he moves like the lotus upon water, touched but unstained.

Such equipoise is possible because the devotee is सङ्गविवर्जितः saṅga-vivarjitaḥ—free from attachment.

This does not mean a heart grown cold or indifferent; rather, it is a heart purified of selfish clinging, able to love without binding, to serve without expectation, and to walk among the shifting sands of life without losing the anchor of divine remembrance.

— ॐ जनकिवल्लभाय नमः ॐ —

Krishna's teaching also clarifies an important subtlety: the love of the devotee is not the worldly love tainted by attachment, which clings possessively or recoils in fear of loss.

Rather it is a love that flows from the realization of Oneness: that there is God in all—a love untainted by self-interest, a love that mirrors the boundless, impartial compassion of the Divine Himself.

In this way, the devotee embodies the mystery of perfect love and perfect freedom intertwined.

— ॐ परब्रह्मणे नमः ॐ —

Krishna invites the aspirant to rise beyond mere outer renunciation or stoic self-control and to cultivate an inner renunciation, where attachment falls away and the heart rests in the sweet stillness of divine peace.

As Krishna's description further unfolds in the next verse, we are drawn ever deeper into the fragrance of this exalted state, where human life is transformed into a transparent vessel of God's love and wisdom.

## *Verse 12.19*

— ॐ श्रीगर्भाय नमः ॐ —

In verse 12.19, Bhagwāna Shri Krishna crowns His description of the beloved devotee with a portrait of serene detachment and inner luminosity.

The devotee is तुल्यनिन्दास्तुति tulya-nindā-stutiḥ—one who takes both reproach and praise alike.

Ordinary minds tremble before the world's judgments, craving approval and shrinking from criticism, but the realized devotee has gone beyond this.

Having cast aside identification with name and form, he no longer sees himself through the eyes of others; he dwells in the silent majesty of the Self, to whom praise and blame are but passing shadows.

— ॐ धन्विने नमः ॐ —

He is मौनी maunī, not merely one who outwardly restrains speech, but one whose mind has entered into the stillness of Oneness.

True मौन mauna is not the muting of the tongue while the mind chatters within; it is the cessation of the inner noise of desire, fear, and wandering thought, leaving the mind absorbed in the remembrance of the Beloved.

Such a one may speak, may even teach, yet his words rise from silence, and his silence is full of the music of God.

— ॐ सत्यभामापतये नमः ॐ —

सन्तुष्टो येन केनचित् santusṭaḥ yena kenacit—content with whatever comes. Whether in abundance or lack, comfort or discomfort, he remains inwardly full, for his joy is not dependent on what arrives or departs.

His heart has drunk the nectar of divine love; no worldly gain can add to it, and no worldly loss can diminish it.

अनिकेतः aniketaḥ—without fixed dwelling, or more profoundly, without the sense of possessiveness toward place or home.

Even if he lives in a palace or a hermitage, the devotee does not call anything "mine." His home is wherever God is present—and for him, that is everywhere. He moves lightly through the world, leaving no trace of claim or bondage.

— ॐ सत्यवाचे नमः ॐ —

Finally, Krishna seals the picture with the most essential quality: भक्तिमान् bhaktimān, full of bhakti.

It is not dry detachment, nor mere stoicism, that makes this being dear to the Lord—it is that all renunciation is pervaded by love.

His equanimity is not cold, but warm with divine presence. His freedom is not emptiness, but fullness in the One he loves above all.

— ॐ श्रीसीतारक्षाय नमः ॐ —

As Krishna concludes this great section of the Bhagavad-Gītā, it becomes clear that these qualities are not only marks of the perfected soul but shining ideals for the aspirant.

Even if one has not yet reached this summit, one is called to walk in that direction—to cultivate contentment, selflessness, and devotion in daily life.

In the final concluding verse, Krishna will tenderly gather together all these marks, honoring both the perfected devotees and those who strive toward these qualities with steadfast love and faith.

— ॐ तत सत ॐ —

Before we move on, let us bow in reverence to this sacred verse. Write it by hand, reflect on its meaning, chant it aloud, make it your own.

— ॐ —

समः शत्रौ च मित्रे च तथा मानापमानयोः ।
samaḥ śatrau ca mitre ca tathā mānāpamānayoḥ
शीतोष्णसुखदुःखेषु समः सङ्गविवर्जितः ॥१२-१८॥
śītoṣṇasukhaduḥkheṣu samaḥ saṅgavivarjitaḥ (12-18)
तुल्यनिन्दास्तुतिर्मौनी सन्तुष्टो येन केनचित् ।
tulyanindāstutirmaunī santuṣṭo yena kenacit
अनिकेतः स्थिरमतिर्भक्तिमान्मे प्रियो नरः ॥१२-१९॥
aniketaḥ sthiramatirbhaktimānme priyo naraḥ (12-19)

— ॐ —

समः शत्रौ च मित्रे च तथा मानापमानयोः ।
samaḥ śatrau ca mitre ca tathā mānāpamānayoḥ
शीतोष्णसुखदुःखेषु समः सङ्गविवर्जितः ॥१२-१८॥
śītoṣṇasukhaduḥkheṣu samaḥ saṅgavivarjitaḥ (12-18)
तुल्यनिन्दास्तुतिर्मौनी सन्तुष्टो येन केनचित् ।
tulyanindāstutirmaunī santuṣṭo yena kenacit
अनिकेतः स्थिरमतिर्भक्तिमान्मे प्रियो नरः ॥१२-१९॥
aniketaḥ sthiramatirbhaktimānme priyo naraḥ (12-19)

ॐ तत्सदिति श्रीमद्भगवद्गीतासूपनिषत्सु ब्रह्मविद्यायां योगशास्त्रे श्रीकृष्णार्जुनसंवादे
om tatsaditi śrīmadbhagavadgītāsūpaniṣatsu brahmavidyāyāṁ yogaśāstre śrīkṛṣṇārjunasaṁvāde
भक्तियोगो नाम द्वादशोऽध्यायः श्लोकः १८-१९
bhaktiyogo nāma dvādaśo'dhyāyaḥ ślokaḥ 18-19

Om-Tat-Sat—Om (Braham) is the sole Reality. In the Yogic Scripture on the Science-of-Braham, the Shrimada-Bhāgvada-Gītā Upanishad, we hereby conclude Shloka 18-19 of the Dialogue between Shrī Krishna and Arjuna entitled Bhakti-Yoga, Canto XII.

## ॐ गीता श्लोकः १२.२० – GĪTĀ VERSE 12.20

ॐ श्रीमद्भगवद्गीतासूपनिषत्सु ब्रह्मविद्यायां योगशास्त्रे श्रीकृष्णार्जुनसंवादे
om śrīmadbhagavadgītāsūpaniṣatsu brahmavidyāyāṁ yogaśāstre śrīkṛṣṇārjunasaṁvāde
भक्तियोगो नाम द्वादशोऽध्यायः श्लोकः २०
bhaktiyogo nāma dvādaśo'dhyāyaḥ ślokaḥ 20

— ॐ —

**ये तु धर्म्यामृतमिदं यथोक्तं पर्युपासते ।**
**ye tu dharmyāmṛtamidaṁ yathoktaṁ paryupāsate**
**श्रद्दधाना मत्परमा भक्तास्तेऽतीव मे प्रियाः** ॥ १२-२० ॥
**śraddadhānā matparamā bhaktāste'tīva me priyāḥ** (12-20)

**Having Me as their supreme goal, these devotees of mine who practice with faith this nectar-like teaching, this ambrosial Dharma which I have just taught—are very dear to Me."** (12.20)

*—: Word-by-Word :—*

ये ye – those who; तु tu – indeed; धर्म्यम् अमृतम् dharmyāmṛtam – this righteous nectar; इदम् idam – this; यथोक्तम् yathoktam – as declared; पर्युपासते paryupāsate – who follow; श्रद्दधानाः śraddadhānāḥ – with faith; मत्-परमाः mat-paramāḥ – who consider me as supreme; भक्ताः bhaktāḥ – devotees; ते te – they; अतीव atīva – exceedingly; मे me – to me; प्रियाः priyāḥ – are dear.

*—: Understanding The Verse :—*

— ॐ श्रीकृष्णाय नमः ॐ —

In this concluding verse of Chapter 12, Bhagwāna Shri Krishna wraps His discourse on devotion with a tender affirmation. Having described in verses 13–19 the noble qualities of the perfected devotee—the one who has realized God—Krishna now turns His gaze to those earnest seekers still journeying toward that sublime goal.

These devotees, who with unwavering faith embrace the teachings He has just given, are described as partaking of the dharmāmṛtam—the nectar of righteousness, the ambrosial path of divine virtues.

— ॐ श्रीरामाय नमः ॐ —

For such souls, Krishna is not merely an object of reverence, but the supreme goal, the center of their love, longing, and surrender.

Krishna assures that these striving aspirants, who persevere with devotion, humility, and faith, are supremely dear to Him.

This verse not only consoles but ennobles the seeker, affirming that one need not wait for 'perfection-reached' to be loved by the Divine; rather, it is the faithful and loving practice itself that draws one closer and closer to the heart of God.

*—: Key Sanskrit Terms :—*

Let us close with the Sanskrit as with a final blessing received at the end of a ritual. "ये तु धर्म्यामृतमिदं यथोक्तं पर्युपासते । श्रद्दधाना मत्परमा भक्तास्तेऽतीव मे प्रियाः ॥ Those who follow this immortal dharma with faith, regarding Me as supreme—such devotees are exceedingly dear to Me." Each word seals the chapter in intimacy, sweetness, and eternal promise.

Come now this is the last verse of the chapter, let us fully explore it; in fact let's be a little playful—roll the Sanskrit on the tongue like sweet fruit, let it burst, let it stain the mouth with something we can't quite name—ambrosia perhaps?

— ॐ —

ये तु (ye tu): "but those who..."

The soft transition तु (tu) sets apart these rare beings — not ordinary aspirants, but those of exceptional spirit who, though in the world, live by a higher law. It marks a distinction: many hear, few truly follow.

— ॐ —

धर्म्यमृतम् (dharmyāmṛtam): "the ambrosial Dharma"

- धर्म्य (dharmya) signifies that which is in perfect accord with Dharma — righteousness, the cosmic order.

- अमृतम् (amṛtam), literally nectar of immortality, reveals that this teaching is not mere ethics, but the very elixir that leads the soul from death to immortality. Here Dharma is not rigid duty, but the living path to eternal life.

— ॐ —

इदं यथोक्तं (idaṁ yathoktaṁ): "this (teaching) as declared"

The Lord emphasizes यथोक्तम् — as I have spoken — underscoring the purity of the teaching.

The wisdom is not to be modified, diluted, or distorted by the mind's preferences. It must be embraced with the sacred humility of a disciple before eternal truth.

— ॐ —

पर्युपासते (paryupāsate): "who devotedly practice and meditate upon"

- उपासना (upāsanā) implies close, reverent meditation, an intimate dwelling upon the teaching until it becomes the very breath and blood of one's being.

The prefix परि- (around, completely) hints at total absorption, not casual practice.

— ॐ —

श्रद्धानाः (śraddadhānāḥ): "endowed with faith"

- श्रद्धा (śraddhā) — that luminous certitude arising not from blind belief but from the deep intuition of truth — is the invisible bridge across the abyss of doubt. It is the soul's quiet trust that what is highest is also most real.

— ॐ —

मत्परमाः (matparamāḥ): "having Me as the Supreme"

Here shines the final jewel.

- परम (parama) means the highest, the beyond.

The devotee who holds the Lord — the infinite, eternal Consciousness — as his sole refuge, his supreme aim, his very life, walks the straightest path to liberation.

— ॐ —

भक्ताः ते अतीव मे प्रियाः (bhaktāḥ te atīva me priyāḥ): "these devotees are exceedingly dear to Me"

- अतीव (atīva) — exceedingly, beyond measure — reveals the intensity of the Lord's love.

This is no mere approval but a profound, overflowing affection, as the ocean rushes to meet the river that has found its way home.

## —: *In Brief* :—

— ॐ श्रीकृष्णाय नमः ॐ —

Bhagwāna Shri Krishna, the supreme refuge of all beings, now offers a final embrace to the striving heart.

Having described the attributes of the perfected devotee—the one who has reached the summit of realization—Krishna now turns to the many who are still climbing, whose steps are unsure but whose hearts are faithful.

These are the devotees who, though not yet perfect, dedicate themselves with reverent faith श्रद्धा (śraddhā) to the practice of these divine virtues and take Krishna as their sole refuge मत्परः (mat-paraḥ), regarding Him as their highest goal, their treasure, their all-in-all.

— ॐ श्रीरामाय नमः ॐ —

Such seekers partake of what Krishna calls धर्म्यम् अमृतम् dharmyāmṛtam—the nectar of righteous wisdom, the immortal teaching that leads to liberation.

This nectar is not merely a set of moral guidelines but the very essence of spiritual transformation; it is the ambrosial path that frees one from death, sorrow, and bondage, drawing the soul into the embrace of the eternal.

Even the attempt to cultivate these qualities—humility, patience, forgiveness, detachment, loving equanimity—is itself a holy act, for it reflects a heart already turning toward God.

— ॐ सौम्याय नमः ॐ —

What is profoundly beautiful here is Krishna's declaration that sincere devotees, are "exceedingly dear" to Him—for they keep endeavoring, drawing nearer with every step, every day—and it matters not if they have attained perfection or not as yet.

A sincere effort is what endears us most to the Lord.

It is not only the one who has arrived at the summit who is beloved, but also the one who climbs with longing, the one who stumbles yet rises again, whose heart beats with the desire to know, love, and serve the Supreme.

Krishna, as the embodiment of compassion, becomes indebted to such love—not because He lacks anything, but because divine love is drawn irresistibly to sincerity and surrender.

— श्रीरामाय नमः —

This verse offers both reassurance and invitation: reassurance to the aspirant who fears falling short, and invitation to all who long for God, assuring them that no honest effort is wasted, no tear unnoticed, no act of devotion unseen.

The seeker who drinks this nectar of wisdom, who aligns his life with the virtues Krishna has outlined, gradually becomes transformed into the image of the Beloved, until the distinction between lover and Loved dissolves into union.

With this, Krishna beautifully concludes His reply to Arjuna's inquiry that began at verse-1 about the highest form of worship. Having honored both the perfected and the striving souls, Krishna leaves the listener with the assurance that the path of devotion is open to all, and that our every step taken with faith and love draws His infinite heart nearer to us.

— ॐ तत सत ॐ —

**Before we move on, let us bow in reverence to this sacred verse. Write it by hand, reflect on its meaning, chant it aloud, make it your own.**

— ॐ —

**ये तु धर्म्यामृतमिदं यथोक्तं पर्युपासते ।**
**ye tu dharmyāmṛtamidaṁ yathoktaṁ paryupāsate**
**श्रद्दधाना मत्परमा भक्तास्तेऽतीव मे प्रियाः ॥ १२-२० ॥**
**śraddadhānā matparamā bhaktāste'tīva me priyāḥ (12-20)**

ये तु धर्म्यामृतमिदं यथोक्तं पर्युपासते ।
ye tu dharmyāmṛtamidaṁ yathoktaṁ paryupāsate
श्रद्दधाना मत्परमा भक्तास्तेऽतीव मे प्रियाः ॥ १२-२० ॥
śraddadhānā matparamā bhaktāste'tīva me priyāḥ (12-20)

ॐ तत्सदिति श्रीमद्भगवद्गीतासूपनिषत्सु ब्रह्मविद्यायां योगशास्त्रे श्रीकृष्णार्जुनसंवादे
om tatsaditi śrīmadbhagavadgītāsūpaniṣatsu brahmavidyāyāṁ yogaśāstre śrīkṛṣṇārjunasaṁvāde
भक्तियोगो नाम द्वादशोऽध्यायः श्लोकः २०
bhaktiyogo nāma dvādaśo'dhyāyaḥ ślokaḥ 20

**Om-Tat-Sat—Om (Braham) is the sole Reality. In the Yogic Scripture on the Science-of-Braham, the Shrimada-Bhāgvada-Gītā Upanishad, we hereby conclude Shloka 20 of the Dialogue between Shrī Krishna and Arjuna entitled Bhakti-Yoga, Canto XII.**

— ॐ पुरुषोत्तमाय नमः ॐ —

The Striver's Crown — Becomes the Beloved of the Lord

O trembling soul, lift up thy gaze —
For the Lord now speaks directly to thee.
Not to some sage retired in mountaintop stillness,
But to the Karma-Yogi who falters, tries, falters, tries—but never quits.

Krishna sees thy tears, thy quiet vows,
Thy silent wrestling in a dark night seemingly endless,
And He reaches out to thee with these special personal words:
"Having Me as the supreme goal,
Ye who drink this धर्म अमृतम dharma-amratam
—The nectar of My ancient words—
This ambrosial Gitā-Dharma which I have taught,
who practice with faith this nectarous teaching
thou always stay most dear to Me,
And I watch over thee most closely!"

# ॐ CHAPTER-TWELVE RECAP

— ॐ तत सत ॐ —

We are at the close of Chapter-Twelve Bhakti Yoga, so let us take a pause to reflect on the gentle, luminous wisdom which Bhagwāna Shri Krishna has poured in this canto—a wisdom that speaks directly to the heart.

This chapter has proven to be a turning point. After the sweeping revelations of divine power and cosmic form in Chapter-Eleven, the Gītā has now drawn us inward. The thunder of metaphysical grandeur has become softened into the quiet music of love, humility, and surrender. Here, the Infinite Himself meets us in the most personal way—as the Beloved who simply asks for our heart and nothing else.

In just twenty verses, Chapter-Twelve brings the loftiest spiritual ideals down to the level of daily life and human relationship. It teaches that God is not only a cosmic force but also a divine friend and beloved— fully approachable through love, humility, and simplicity of heart.

— ॐ —

Let us now sum up the salient points of Chapter-Twelve:

Two Paths to the Divine: With Form and Without

Krishna begins by addressing a core spiritual question: Should one worship the formless, unmanifest Absolute (nirguṇa brahman) or the personal God (saguṇa īśvara)?

While both are valid, Krishna affirms that the path of devotion to the personal Divine is more accessible, especially for those still embodied, bound by mind and senses. It is a path infused with grace.

A Compassionate Ladder of Spiritual Progress

Recognizing that not everyone can instantly fix the mind on God with unwavering love, Krishna gently offers a series of progressive options:

- If you can, focus your mind and intellect on Me
- If not, practice daily remembrance and devotion
- If that feels distant, act selflessly for My sake
- If even that is difficult, renounce the fruits of your actions

In these steps, we see Krishna's compassion—a Divine Teacher who lowers the ladder to meet the seeker at every stage.

**The Inner Mark of a Devotee**

The heart of the chapter lies in its description of the qualities dear to Krishna. The true devotee is not defined by rituals or external renunciation, but by inward transformation:

- Freedom from hatred, pride, and possessiveness
- Compassion and gentleness
- Equanimity in joy and sorrow, success and failure
- Contentment, humility, and nonviolence
- An unwavering mind rooted in the Divine

These are not abstract ideals—they are living qualities that grow in the soil of sincere devotion. Such a devotee, Krishna says again and again, is dear to Me.

**Love Above All**

Above all, Chapter-Twelve affirms that what matters most is love—not perfection, not ritual mastery, not intellectual brilliance, but a heart sincerely offered. The path of bhakti is not about what we do, but how we do it—with love, surrender, and remembrance of the Divine.

**Looking Ahead**

With Chapter-Twelve, the Gītā completes a central arc of its teaching—moving from action (karma), to knowledge (jñāna), and now, to devotion (bhakti).

— ॐ —

In the chapters that follow, beginning with Chapter-Thirteen, Krishna will return to metaphysical analysis, dissecting the nature of reality, the body and the soul, the three guṇas, and the workings of prakṛti (nature).

But even as the teaching becomes more philosophical, the spirit of Chapter-Twelve will remain a steady undercurrent: whatever knowledge we gain, whatever action we perform—without devotion, the journey remains incomplete.

**Final Thought**

In a world full of striving, comparison, and confusion, Chapter-Twelve offers quiet reassurance:

- We do not have to be perfect—just stay present before Krishna.
- We do not have to understand everything—just love Krishna sincerely.
- And in that love, the Divine draws near, saying: "You are dear to Me."

This chapter stands as a beacon for all us seekers—whether one's temperament leans toward knowledge, action, or meditation; it teaches that the heart's sincere devotion remains the truest offering.

ॐ तत्सदिति श्रीमद्भगवद्गीतासूपनिषत्सु ब्रह्मविद्यायां योगशास्त्रे श्रीकृष्णार्जुनसंवादे
om tatsaditi śrīmadbhagavadgītāsūpaniṣatsu brahmavidyāyāṁ yogaśāstre śrīkṛṣṇārjunasaṁvāde
भक्तियोगो नाम द्वादशोऽध्यायः ॥
bhaktiyogo nāma dvādaśo'dhyāyaḥ .

Om-Tat-Sat—Om (Braham) is the sole Reality. In this Yogic Scripture on the Science of Brahama—the Shrimada-Bhāgvada-Gītā Upanishad—hereby ends the dialogue between Shrī Krishna and Arjuna entitled: Bhakti Yoga, Canto XII.

— श्रीसीतामनोरमाय नमः —

O mortal, attend to the Lord's lucid words,
Canto Twelve is Krishna's deep voice with smile to calm all doubts,
For here He speaks direct to thee—the earnest-heart Karma-Yogi.

Lifting His voice like a song across dawn, Krishna proclaims the Word:
"Given to contemplation, they whose hearts stay fixed on Me,
Who worship Me with love that never wanes,
Unflinching, Content, Detached, Ever-Equanimous, Beyond-Dualities.
Whose faith, like the mountain, holds firm through every storm—
These are the Yogis most dear to Me!"
O Soul, incline thine ear, hear the Lord's proclamation—and rejoice!

Beloved of Krishna—Yes;
But the true Yogi is not exactly the darling of the world.
Times have changed too much— today he is laughed at and hounded.
In this age, the Karma-Yogi will stay unknown, unsung—
But worse, he will be trampled into the ground,
scorned, disdained, spurned by scoundrels of the world—
— To him it matters not—doesn't even figure on his vision horizon.

That Real-Hero, that true Karma-Yogi, is Dear—
—Not to kings, not to crowds, not to the world—
But he is "...Most-dear to Me..."— says Krishna,
"He has none and nothing—but Me;
and that is enough qualification."
Staying raised in the eyes of Shri Krishna—that's all which really counts.

— ॐ तत सत ॐ —

—————————ॐ—————————

ॐ ॐ ॐ ॐ ॐ ॐ ॐ ॐ ॐ ॐ ॐ ॐ ॐ ॐ ॐ ॐ ॐ

## ॐ गीतामाहात्म्यम् GĪTĀ-MĀHĀTMYAM

[ Verses on the glory and import of the Bhagavad-Gītā ]

— ॐ —

गीताशास्त्रमिदं पुण्यं यः पठेत्प्रयतः पुमान् ।
gītāśāstramidaṁ puṇyaṁ yaḥ paṭhetprayataḥ pumān ,
विष्णोः पदमवाप्नोति भयशोकादिवर्जितः ॥
viṣṇoḥ padamavāpnoti bhayaśokādivarjitaḥ .

**One who diligently studies this Bhagavad-Gītā—the bestower of all virtues—with firm devotion and a regulated mind—verily attains Vaikuntha—the holy abode of Māhā-Vishnu—and he stands freed of all the fears and sorrows of this mundane world.**

— ॐ —

गीताध्ययनशीलस्य प्राणायामपरस्य च ।
gītādhyayanaśīlasya prāṇāyāmaparasya ca ,
नैव सन्ति हि पापानि पूर्वजन्मकृतानि च ॥
naiva santi hi pāpāni pūrvajanmakṛtāni ca .

**One who performs Prāṇāyāms and studies the Bhagavad-Gītā regularly and sincerely—all his sins melt away, even those from all prior lives.**

— ॐ —

मलनिर्मोचनं पुंसां जलस्नानं दिने दिने ।
malanirmocanaṁ puṁsāṁ jalasnānaṁ dine dine ,
सकृद्गीताम्भसि स्नानं संसारमलनाशनम् ॥
sakṛdgītāmbhasi snānaṁ saṁsāramalanāśanam .

**A daily bath removes external bodily taints, but a single bath in the sacred waters of Bhagavad-Gītā is enough to remove all the taints of this Saṁsāra—this polluting worldly existence of joys, sorrows, births, and deaths.**

— ॐ —

गीता सुगीता कर्तव्या किमन्यैः शास्त्रविस्तरैः ।
gītā sugītā kartavyā kimanyaiḥ śāstravistaraiḥ ,
या स्वयं पद्मनाभस्य मुखपद्माद्विनिःसृता ॥
yā svayaṁ padmanābhasya mukhapadmādviniḥsṛtā .

**Why go in for other elaborate scriptures, when you can chant the Gītā—the essence of all Vedic scriptures—which issued forth from the lotus mouth of Māhā-Vishnu Himself—on whose navel is the lotus of Creation.**

— ॐ —

भारतामृतसर्वस्वं विष्णोर्वक्त्राद्विनिःसृतम् ।
bhāratāmṛtasarvasvaṁ viṣṇorvaktrādviniḥsṛtam ,
गीतागङ्गोदकं पीत्वा पुनर्जन्म न विद्यते ॥
gītāgaṅgodakaṁ pītvā punarjanma na vidyate .

**There is no more rebirth for one who partakes of the sacred waters of the Gītā-Gangā—the holy stream which flowed out from the lotus lips of Shri Māhā-Vishnu—the nectar which is the quintessence of Māhā-Bhārata.**

— ॐ —

एकं शास्त्रं देवकीपुत्रगीतमेको देवो देवकीपुत्र एव ।
ekaṁ śāstraṁ devakīputragītameko devo devakīputra eva ,
एको मन्त्रस्तस्य नामानि यानि कर्माप्येकं तस्य देवस्य सेवा ॥
eko mantrastasya nāmāni yāni karmāpyekaṁ tasya devasya sevā .

**The holy Gītā of Krishna—son of Devakī—is the One Scripture; Krishna—son of Devakī—is the One God; the name Krishna—son of Devakī—is the One Mantra; service to Him—son of Devakī—is the One and only Duty.**

— ॐ —

श्रीकृष्णचरणार्पणमस्तु
śrī kṛṣṇa caraṇāarpaṇamastu
Hereby dedicated to the Lotus Feet of Bhagwāna Shri Krishna.

कायेन वाचा मनसेंद्रियैर्वा । बुद्ध्यात्मना वा प्रकृतिस्वभावात् ।
kāyena vācā manaseṁdriyairvā , buddhyātmanā vā prakritisvabhāvāt ,
करोमि यद्यत् सकलं परस्मै । नारायणायेति समर्पयामि ॥
karomi yadyat sakalaṁ parasmai , nārāyaṇāyeti samarpayāmi .

**Whatever it is I do—through body, mind, speech, or sense-organs, or with my intellect and soul, or with my innate natural tendencies—whatever it be—I offer it all unto Narayana (Bhagwāna Shri Krishna / Bhagwāna Shri Rāma).**

— ॐ —

**या गीता सनातनस्य धर्मस्यामृतरूपिणी।**
**yā gītā sanātanasya dharmasyāmṛtarūpiṇī ,**
**लोकानां मार्गदर्शिनी तस्याः मूलं प्रयच्छामि ॥**
**lokānāṁ margadarśinī tasyāḥ mūlaṁ prayacchāmi .**

That Gītā, which's the nectar-form of Sanātana Dharma—the guide of the worlds upon The-Path—towards Her sacred roots I now proceed to take refuge.



*Be Inspired and Inspire Others. Light a Lamp of Wisdom.*
*Start your own Gītā Classes with a Friend Today.*

www.ingramcontent.com/pod-product-compliance
Lightning Source LLC
Chambersburg PA
CBHW081431070526
44586CB00020B/2550
*9781945739521*